W9-BIY-542

Myra Waldo's
Chinese Cookbook

ILLUSTRATED BY *Rosalie Petrash*

THE MACMILLAN COMPANY, NEW YORK

COLLIER-MACMILLAN LTD., LONDON

Library of Congress Catalog Card Number: 68-17205

SECOND PRINTING 1968

The Macmillan Company, New York
Collier-Macmillan Canada Ltd., Toronto, Ontario

Printed in the United States of America

Contents

Introduction

If there are three great cuisines in the world, as gourmets claim, there can be little doubt that they are the French, Italian and Chinese. Many experts believe that the Chinese is not the least of the three.

First of all, what is Chinese cooking? How does it differ from Western cookery styles? It should be remembered that China is a vast, teeming, overpopulated country where the raising of food has always been a great problem. Except for a fortunate few, the Chinese have to work long hours in order to obtain enough to eat for themselves and their families. Many thousands of years ago, rice became the dietary mainstay of a large part of the population of China, but although most Westerners are not aware of it, an equally large number of Chinese subsist upon barley, wheat and other cereals. Much of the nation's cuisine, however, is centered about rice. Also, at a time when the civilized world in the West knew nothing of the benefits obtained from eating plants or concerned itself with vitamins, the Chinese were basing their cookery on vegetables.

With a daily income per person reckoned in the equivalent of American pennies, the Chinese housewife has developed shopping and cooking methods quite different from our own. Usually there is enough rice for the family, but the problem lies in giving it variety and flavor so that the meals will be as interesting as possible. The Chinese do not think of whole roasts of meat, entire chickens or ducks (for these are far beyond their means), but rather in terms of tiny quantities of poultry or meat to be used to add flavor and variety to the basic rice and vegetables. To achieve this, the Chinese housewife may buy as little as an ounce of pork, an equal amount of chicken, and possibly a third infinitesimal quantity of duck. It is precisely this inventiveness and ingenuity that has created the entire realm of Chinese cookery with its seemingly endless variety of dishes.

Chinese families follow the three-meals-a-day pattern of the Western world, but what they consider a meal has little resemblance to a Western menu. Breakfast, as a rule, consists of a gruel, boiled rice (congee) or boiled noodles. "Lunch" is made up of a number of different dishes, three or four at a minimum, plus rice and perhaps a soup. Tea is not served during a meal, but at its conclusion. The evening meal is similar to the midday meal, but the dishes are never repeated, nor are they likely to be repeated for several weeks if the cook is competent. The Chinese never make a single dish into a complete main course, and all but the very poorest Chinese families will make an effort to have several main-course dishes. Therefore, when a recipe in this book specifies that it serves four, for example, it is on the assumption that several other dishes will be served; otherwise, the quantity specified will be sufficient for only two persons.

Just as the United States has a variety of cooking styles (Southern, Pennsylvania Dutch, Creole, New England, etc.), so do the Chinese recognize a dozen or more different regional styles of preparing food. But the great difference in Chinese cooking lies in the fact that any one particular local cuisine consists of literally thousands of dishes, a variety which demonstrates an amazing ingenuity. Of all the provincial cooking styles, however, the experts usually select as outstanding those of Shantung, Fukien, Honan, Szechwan, and, of course, Canton.

Beginning with the province of Shantung, we find that, with one exception, the dishes of this region are little known in our country, for they are not served in the majority of Chinese restaurants here. The exception is duck, which is found occasionally in places that feature "Peking" cooking, which, more accurately, should be called "Shantung," for Peking itself has no authentic cookery style.

Fukien, the region of the Yangtze River delta, features noodles and other dough preparations. The province of Honan specializes in sweet-and-sour dishes. Szechwan food is very highly seasoned, often with hot peppers. This cuisine also contains a variety of salty dishes. Only a very few Chinese restaurants, in New York, Chicago and San Francisco, feature this unusual cookery style.

As we all know, it is Cantonese cooking that has made the greatest impact upon the United States. The vast majority of our Chinese restaurants are Cantonese, and the largest number of dishes on their menus are Cantonese in origin. While Cantonese cooking is extremely good, and quite varied, it is not better than that of the other provinces mentioned above. Why, then, does Cantonese cooking have such a strong influence upon Chinese cooking as found in the United States? The precise reasons are not completely clear, but it is true that the greatest number of Chinese immigrants to our shores were recruited from Canton, about the time of the California Gold Rush of 1849, a little over a century ago. They came to work on the railroads of the Western United States, chiefly on the Union Pacific Railroad, then under construction. The labor recruiters brought along also the Cantonese cooks, for they correctly guessed that the Chinese workmen would not care to eat the Western fare served to the American laborers. When the railroads were finished, the Chinese drifted into other work—farming, ranching, laundering—and, of course, they opened restaurants. In the beginning, these small restaurants were intended to serve only local residents of a community, but eating Chinese food became a great American fad, then a habit.

Chinese food is enormously, almost unbelievably, popular in our country. In the smallest town there is likely to be a Chinese restaurant; in the larger cities there are sure to be scores, sometimes even hundreds. New York City has at least two thousand Chinese restaurants by the latest count—an outstanding example of the popularity of Chinese food.

How to Cook
in the Chinese Style

Authentic Chinese cooking places its emphasis upon preparation, rather than upon cooking procedure. Everything is carefully prepared before cooking is started, so that the actual cooking is a swift, smooth operation taking, "for the most part, a very short time," often only a few minutes. For this reason, and because Chinese cookery represents a decided departure from the usual American style, the beginner is strongly urged to begin by preparing only one Chinese dish at a time. After this has been carried off successfully and becomes a part of the repertoire, a second dish may be attempted. After a few successes, it will then be possible to prepare complete Chinese dinners of complexity and subtlety for your family and friends.

But first, we strongly urge that you read over the following instructions at least twice before beginning to cook in the Chinese style.

Slicing and chopping are of the utmost importance. Meats should be sliced quite thin, often paper-thin, and cut into pieces that usually measure about 1 by 2 inches. Slice meat against the grain, that is, at right angles to the direction of the meat fibers.

Vegetable slicing is a fine art, too. Firm vegetables such as celery, Chinese cabbage, asparagus, and the like, are always sliced diagonally, for this method exposes a greater surface area to the heat and the juices in the pan. This permits these vegetables to cook much more quickly than they ordinarily would. Tender vegetables, however, are sliced vertically. For example, green onions and mushrooms are sliced straight up and down, for these cook quickly.

When the recipe calls for *diced* food, try to make the dice small and as nearly the same size as possible; this will permit them to cook evenly, so that all of the diced foods will have the same texture. Truly skillful cooks dice so meticulously that each edge looks as if it were cut by a machine.

When meat is to be cut into *chunks*, the pieces should be cut much larger, in squares up to 1 inch, but the size will generally be specified in the particular recipe.

Except for duck and a few other specialties that require advance preparation, don't begin to cook until everyone is just about ready to eat, because, we repeat, Chinese cookery is usually a very brief affair, often a matter of only five minutes or so. A first important step is to assemble all of the ingredients needed in the recipe, because it would be disastrous to the dish if you had to stop to search for a particular ingredient during the cooking process.

If possible, invest in a Chinese *wok*. This is a circular two-handled iron pan, shallow enough for pan frying, yet deep enough for fricasseeing and deep frying. Unlike the heavy frying pan found in most American kitchens, the *wok* is relatively thin. This and the rounded bottom permit the quick concentrated heat required for most Chinese cooking. The rounded bottom also does away with corners for food to get stuck in and burned, and makes stirring easier. If a *wok* isn't available, use an ordinary skillet, or frying pan.

Cook with fresh vegetable or peanut oil; butter, margarine or olive oil, on the other hand, are completely unsuitable. Sometimes lard may be used. Heat the amount of oil specified in the recipe until it is quite hot, being careful not to add any ingredients until it is well heated. Speed is essential in Chinese cookery, so it is important never to leave the pan. Have available a stirrer of some sort (chopsticks are excellent for this purpose), because as the foods cook, they should be constantly stirred. The stirring phase is *most* important when the ingredients are first added, because the stirring coats them with oil and seals their natural juices. This cookery style is called *stir-frying*, and is the method used in many Chinese dishes.

Chinese food must be served hot, and this means that it must be served immediately. *Do not overcook* Chinese food, and do not exceed the cooking times specified in the recipes. The vegetables in some dishes may, at first, seem slightly undercooked to Western palates, but this is intentionally done, for the Chinese cuisine places strong emphasis upon crisp, crunchy foods.

Learn how to prepare perfect rice. This is important, for almost all Chinese meals have rice as their basis. Do not serve Western bread with Chinese food, for it will be completely out of place. There is, however, a Chinese bread (see recipe, page 73) that complements many of the dishes. Most stores carry China tea, and this will complete the effect of an authentic Chinese meal.

Note about the number of persons each recipe will serve:
In Chinese cooking, there are always several main courses. When a recipe in this book specifies that it will (for example) serve four, it is on the assumption that more than one main course will be served. Suggested menus are given at the end of the book.

A Few Notes about Chinese Ingredients

Nowadays the most frequently used Chinese ingredients are available in supermarkets and delicatessens throughout the country. There are, however, a few ingredients which must be obtained from a Chinese grocer or importer (a partial list of these sources is given below). It is always better to work with fresh Chinese vegetables if you can obtain them, so if your city has a Chinese market section, a trip there is well worth the effort.

Bamboo shoots may be obtained fresh only in Chinese food markets, but canned bamboo shoots are excellent and readily available.

Bean curd is made from ground soy-bean paste, water and calcium sulphate. It has a fine white texture resembling custard. It is available only from a Chinese food market, and it must be kept refrigerated.

Bean sprouts are available fresh only in Chinese food markets, but canned bean sprouts are readily available in supermarkets. You can also grow them yourself from dried mung peas (see recipe, page 147, in the Vegetable section).

Black beans are small oval black beans the size of a pea. They come in bags or packages.

Broth, as called for in these recipes, refers to a home-made chicken or beef broth (either may be used), but canned broth is equally acceptable. Do not use bouillon cubes, however; they are too salty.

Cellophane noodles are transparent noodles made from ground mung peas and cut thin like threads. They are available in packages.

Chinese brown sauce, or *chiang,* is a condiment made from red kidney beans and is available in bottles in supermarkets.

Chinese dried mushrooms, available in supermarkets, are dark brown in color and have a more pronounced flavor than fresh mushrooms. Before using, soak in warm water 30 minutes to soften. Use the soaking water as additional liquid in sauces.

Five-spice powder is a combination of ground cinnamon, cloves, peppercorns, fennel and anise. It is especially good for seasoning pork and duck. It is available from specialty shops or Chinese food markets.

Hoisin sauce is a thick reddish sauce made of hot chili peppers, soybeans, sugar and flour and used for flavoring other sauces. It is available in bottles and cans from specialty shops or Chinese food markets.

Peanut, vegetable or sesame-seed oil are used in these recipes. If you wish, use lard. However, butter or margarine should not be used.

Monosodium glutamate is an almost tasteless, vaguely salty powder used to enhance the flavor of foods. It is most commonly marketed as Ac'cent or M.S.G.

Oyster sauce is useful in sauces for meat, fish or poultry. This combination of oysters with herbs and spices is available in bottles or cans in supermarkets.

Snow-pea pods are available frozen from the supermarket. If you buy them fresh from a Chinese grocery, trim the end tips.

Soy sauce is found in a large proportion of Chinese recipes, replacing most of the salt customarily required in American cooking.

Rice, as used in Chinese recipes, is the long-grain (unconverted) variety.

Water chestnuts are sweet, juicy and crisp. They are used as a vegetable and usually sliced and added to dishes for texture and flavor. They are available in jars or cans in most supermarkets. In season, fresh unpeeled water chestnuts are sold by the pound in Chinese grocery stores.

Sources for Chinese Ingredients

Arizona

Phoenix Produce Company
202 South 3rd Street
Phoenix

Tang's Market
4102 North 24th Street
Phoenix

Soleng's
2320 South 6th Street
Tucson

California

Co-op Shopping Centers
1414 University Avenue or 1550 Shattuck Avenue
Berkeley

U-Save Center Market
1654 University Avenue
Berkeley

Kwong On Lung, Importers
686 North Spring Street
Los Angeles

Yee Sing Chong Company
950 Castelan Street
Los Angeles

Wing Chong Company
367 8th Street
Oakland

S. P. Depot Market
310 "I" Street
Sacramento

Ginn Fat Company
953 Grant Avenue
San Francisco

Mow Lee Shing Kee Company
774 Commercial Street
San Francisco

Illinois

Man Sun Wing Company
2229 Wentworth Avenue
Chicago

Mee Jun Mercantile Company
2223 Wentworth Avenue
Chicago

Sun Wah Hing Trading Company
2246 Wentworth Avenue
Chicago

Massachusetts

Sun Sun Company
340 Oxford Street
Boston

Tai Kwong Company
60 Beach Street
Boston

Michigan

Lun Yick Company
1339 3rd Avenue
Detroit

New York

Cathay Food Products
115 Broadway
New York City

Eastern Trading Co., Inc.
2801 Broadway
New York City

Oriental Food Shop
1302 Amsterdam Avenue
New York City

Wing Fat Company
35 Mott Street
New York City

Wing Woh Lung
50 Mott Street
New York City

Ohio
Sun Lee Yuen Company
1726 Payne Avenue
Cleveland

Oregon
Fong Chong Company
301 N.W. 4th Avenue
Portland

Texas
Chung Hing
202 Milam Street
Houston

Oriental Import-Export Company
2009 Polk Street
Houston

Taiwan Importing Company
1716 Texas Avenue
Houston

Adler's
2012 Broadway
San Antonio

Washington (state)
Wah Young Company
717 S. King Street
Seattle

Ken's Supermarket
9132 Veterans Drive
Tacoma

Thriftway Supermarket
Villa Plaza
Tacoma

Washington, D.C.
Mee Wah Lung Company
608 H Street, N.W.

Appetizers

1

Appetizers

Chinese Mustard and Duck (Plum) Sauce are custom-arily served with Chinese dishes. They are both readily available in jars, but since they are so easy to make at home, I give the recipes below.

Chinese Mustard

½ cup dry Chinese or English mustard
boiled water, cooled

Mix the mustard with spoonfuls of water, stirring steadily until smooth and the consistency you like. The Chinese prefer mustard somewhat runny.

Duck (Plum) Sauce

A Suitable Substitute

½ cup chutney   1 tablespoon sugar
1 cup plum jam   1 tablespoon vinegar

Chop the chutney very fine. Mix with the plum jam, sugar and vinegar.

Makes about 1½ cups.

Barbecued Spareribs

½ cup honey
½ cup soy sauce
1½ cups beef broth
3 tablespoons cider
     vinegar
2 tablespoons dry sherry

2 cloves garlic, minced
1 tablespoon sugar
1 teaspoon ground ginger
2 racks spareribs (about
     4 pounds), cracked

Combine the honey, soy sauce, beef broth, vinegar, sherry, garlic, sugar and ginger in a bowl. Add the spareribs and marinate at room temperature 2 hours, turning and basting frequently. Drain, reserving marinade. Arrange ribs on a rack in a shallow roasting pan and roast in a 350° oven 1¼ hours, basting frequently with marinade and pouring off accumulated fat. To serve, cut into individual ribs.

(SERVES 8–10.

Garlic Spareribs

1 rack spareribs (about
     2 pounds)
6 cloves garlic
1 slice ginger root or ¼
     teaspoon ground ginger
½ teaspoon cinnamon

½ teaspoon anise
1½ teaspoons salt
1½ teaspoons sugar
½ cup soy sauce
2 tablespoons dry sherry

Wash and dry the spareribs. Crush the garlic or put through a press. Mix with the ginger, cinnamon, anise, salt, sugar, soy sauce and sherry. Brush over both sides of the spareribs and let stand 1 hour. Brush frequently with any leftover marinade.

Fill a roasting pan with boiling water. Place a rack over it (not touching water) and put the spareribs on it. Roast in a 400° oven 45 minutes. To serve, cut into individual ribs.

❲ SERVES 2–4.

Barbecued Pork

2 *pork tenderloins (about*
   2 *pounds)*
⅔ *cup soy sauce*
¼ *cup dry sherry*
2 *cloves garlic, minced*

2 *green onions, chopped*
4 *thin slices ginger root or 1*
   teaspoon ground ginger ·
3 *tablespoons honey*
1 *tablespoon sugar*

If pork tenderloin is not available, buy a pork butt and cut it lengthwise into 2-inch-wide strips. A 6-rib boneless loin of pork, cut lengthwise into 2-inch-wide strips, may also be used.

Combine the soy sauce, sherry, garlic, green onion and ginger root. Marinate the meat in the mixture 12 hours or overnight. Drain. Rub pork strips with a mixture of the honey and sugar. Place on a greased rack and roast in a 375° oven 20 minutes. Reduce heat to 300° and roast 20 minutes longer, turning the meat once. Slice thin and serve hot or cold. Serve with mustard.

❲ SERVES 8–10.

Marinated Pork with Sesame Seeds

2 *pork tenderloins (about*
   2 *pounds)*
¾ *cup soy sauce*
5 *tablespoons sugar*
¼ *cup beef broth*

½ *teaspoon black pepper*
1 *teaspoon ground ginger*
2 *cloves garlic*
½ *cup sesame seeds*

Trim the pork of all fat. (If tenderloins are not available, loin of pork, boned and cut in long, narrow strips may be used.)

In a bowl, combine the soy sauce, sugar, broth, pepper, ginger, garlic and sesame seeds. Marinate the pork in the mixture for 3 hours at room temperature. Turn and baste the meat frequently. Lift meat out and place on a baking pan. Roast in a 350° oven 45 minutes, turning and basting meat frequently. Cut in diagonal slices.

([SERVES 6–8.

Chicken in Papers

2 *whole chicken breasts,*   ¼ *cup minced green onion*
  skinned and boned   2 *teaspoons dry sherry*
3 *tablespoons soy sauce*   ¼ *teaspoon ground ginger*
1 *tablespoon vegetable oil*   ⅛ *teaspoon cinnamon*
½ *cup minced mushrooms*   *vegetable oil for deep frying*
3 *water chestnuts, chopped*

Put skinned and boned chicken breasts between 2 sheets of waxed paper and pound as thin as possible. Cut chicken into 3-inch-square pieces and sprinkle with 2 tablespoons soy sauce. Let stand 10 minutes. Heat the oil in a skillet and sauté the mushrooms, water chestnuts and green onions for 3 minutes. Stir in the sherry, ginger, cinnamon and remaining soy sauce. Cool. Spread some of the mixture on one half of each chicken square, fold over and press edges together. Cut parchment paper, waxed paper or aluminum foil into 4-inch squares and put 1 piece of chicken in the center of each. Fold like an envelope. Chill 2 hours.

Heat the fat to 370° and carefully slide the packages into the fat, a few at a time. Fry 5 minutes. Drain. Serve in the paper.

([MAKES ABOUT 10.

Spiced Chicken Wings

12 *chicken wings*	1 *tablespoon sugar*
2 *cups boiling water*	4 *teaspoons salt*
1 *onion*	½ *teaspoon black pepper*
⅓ *cup oyster sauce*	1½ *tablespoons cinnamon*
3 *tablespoons soy sauce*	1 *teaspoon ground ginger*

Remove any pinfeathers. Cut off the wing tips. Wash and
dry the wings. Cook the wings with the boiling water and
onion 5 minutes. Drain, reserving 1¼ cups of the stock.
Discard the onion. To the reserved stock, add the oyster
sauce, soy sauce and sugar. Add the wings, bring to a boil
and cook over low heat 20 minutes or until tender. Drain,
dry and cool. Combine the salt, pepper, cinnamon and
ginger in a skillet. Heat, shaking the pan, then coat the
wings with the mixture by dipping them into the skillet.

❲ SERVES 6–12.

Egg Rolls

3 *eggs*	2 *teaspoons cornstarch*
1 *teaspoon salt*	3 *tablespoons chopped*
½ *pound ground beef or*	*onion*
pork	3 *tablespoons flour*
2 *teaspoons soy sauce*	3 *tablespoons water*
2 *teaspoons dry sherry*	*vegetable oil for deep frying*
½ *teaspoon ground ginger*	

Beat the eggs with ½ teaspoon salt. Pour about 2 tablespoons into a hot greased 6-inch skillet, tilting the pan
quickly. Fry until lightly browned and set. Repeat with
remaining eggs. You should have 6 egg pancakes.

Combine the ground meat, soy sauce, sherry, ginger,
cornstarch, onion and remaining salt; mix thoroughly.

Divide meat mixture among the egg sheets. Turn opposite sides in and roll up. Seal edges with the flour mixed with the water. Heat the oil to 370° and fry the rolls in it until browned. Drain rolls and cut crosswise on the bias into 3 pieces each. Serve hot, with mixed salt and pepper for dipping, or with mustard.

〖 SERVES 6.

Spring Rolls

PANCAKE

1 *cup sifted flour*   1 *cup water*
2 *eggs*   *vegetable oil*

Beat together the flour, eggs and water until very smooth. Let stand 15 minutes.

Brush a hot 7-inch skillet with a little oil. Pour in 1 tablespoon batter, tilting the pan quickly to coat the bottom. Bake until underside is lightly browned and top dry. Turn out onto a napkin, browned side up. Stack while preparing the balance of the pancakes. Reserve a little batter for sealing the pancakes. Place 2 tablespoons of the filling (see recipe below) on the browned side of each pancake. Spread the filling lengthwise, then fold the pancake edge which is along the length of the filling over the filling, then fold one end over this, then the other end, and finally, moisten the edge of the remaining side with a little batter. Fold this over the roll, pressing the edges together. Fry in deep 370° oil until browned and crisp. Cut each roll into 3 pieces. Serve with Chinese Mustard and Duck Sauce.

〖 MAKES ABOUT 12.

PORK FILLING (FOR SPRING ROLLS)

½ *pound boneless pork*
⅓ *cup vegetable oil*
¾ *teaspoon salt*
1 *teaspoon cornstarch*
1 *tablespoon dry sherry*
¼ *cup thinly sliced green onion*

½ *cup julienne-cut water chestnuts*
½ *cup chopped mushrooms*
½ *cup bean sprouts*
2 *tablespoons soy sauce*

Cut the pork in very thin ½-inch-long pieces. Heat half the oil in a skillet; sauté the pork until browned. Sprinkle with the salt, cornstarch and sherry. Cook over low heat 5 minutes, stirring frequently. Turn mixture into a bowl.

Heat the remaining oil in the skillet; sauté the green onion, water chestnuts, mushrooms and bean sprouts 5 minutes, stirring frequently. Mix in the soy sauce. Add to the pork mixture, mix thoroughly and cool. Proceed as directed.

Pork-Stuffed Clams

24 *cherrystone clams*
½ *cup water*
½ *pound ground pork*
½ *cup finely chopped green onion*
1 *tablespoon soy sauce*

2 *tablespoons dry sherry*
1 *teaspoon sugar*
1 *teaspoon ground ginger*
3 *tablespoons vegetable oil*
½ *cup beef broth*

Wash and scrub the clams until water runs clean. Place in a deep skillet with ½ cup water; cover and cook until shells open. Discard any clams that don't open. Drain, remove the clams and reserve the shells.

Chop the clams, then mix with the pork, green onion, soy sauce, sherry, sugar and ginger. Divide the mixture among the shells. Combine the oil and broth in a baking pan; arrange the clams in it in a single layer. Bake in a 350° oven 20 minutes.

⟪ SERVES 6–8.

Pork-Stuffed Mushrooms

½ *pound raw pork, ground*	1 *tablespoon flour*
¼ *pound raw shrimp,*	1 *teaspoon salt*
shelled and deveined	¼ *teaspoon black pepper*
3 *tablespoons chopped*	24 *large mushrooms*
green onion	1 *cup beef broth*
3 *tablespoons soy sauce*	

Combine the pork, shrimp and green onion and chop very fine. Mix in 1 tablespoon soy sauce, the flour, salt and pepper. Form into small balls. Wash and dry the mushrooms and remove the stems. Stuff with the pork-shrimp balls. Put the remaining soy sauce and the beef broth in a large skillet and arrange the mushrooms in it, stuffed side up. Cover and cook over low heat 20 minutes, or until no pink remains in the pork. Serve as an hors d'oeuvre on small plates, accompanied by forks.

⟪ SERVES 6–8.

Shrimp-Stuffed Mushrooms

12 *Chinese dried, or fresh,*	½ *teaspoon ground ginger*
mushrooms	1 *teaspoon dry sherry*
½ *pound raw shrimp,*	1 *teaspoon cornstarch*
shelled and deveined	1 *egg white*
1 *teaspoon salt*	¼ *cup water*
2 *tablespoons minced green*	2 *tablespoons vegetable oil*
onion	1 *tablespoon soy sauce*

This dish is customarily prepared with Chinese dried mushrooms, but if you can't get them, buy large firm mushrooms. If dried mushrooms are used, soak in lukewarm water for 30 minutes. Drain. If fresh mushrooms are used, wash and dry. Remove the stems of the dried or fresh mushrooms and use for another purpose.

Chop the shrimp very fine and mix with the salt, green onion, ginger, sherry, cornstarch and unbeaten egg white. Stuff the mushrooms. Arrange in a skillet, stuffed side up. Add a mixture of the water, oil and soy sauce. Bring to a boil, cover and cook over low heat 10 minutes. Drain. Serve hot.

❪ MAKES 12.

Shrimp Toast

1 pound shrimp, shelled and deveined
1 teaspoon minced ginger root or ½ teaspoon ground ginger
1 teaspoon dry sherry
1 teaspoon salt
1 egg white
1 teaspoon cornstarch
⅛ teaspoon monosodium glutamate
8 slices bread, trimmed
2 tablespoons chopped ham
2 tablespoons chopped parsley
vegetable oil for deep frying

Chop the shrimp very fine. Mix in the ginger, sherry, salt, unbeaten egg white, cornstarch and monosodium glutamate. Mix thoroughly. Cut each slice of bread into 4 squares and spread some shrimp mixture on each square. Sprinkle the shrimp with ham and parsley and press down lightly. Heat the oil to 370° and fry the squares first with shrimp-mixture side down, then turn over and fry until bread is golden brown. Drain. Serve hot as an hors d'oeuvre.

❪ MAKES 32 SQUARES.

Batter-Fried Shrimp

2 *eggs*	1 *pound raw shrimp,*
½ *teaspoon salt*	*shelled and*
⅛ *teaspoon white pepper*	*deveined*
4 *tablespoons rice flour*	*vegetable oil for deep*
or cornstarch	*frying*

Beat the eggs with the salt, pepper and rice flour. Dip shrimp in this batter, coating well, and fry in hot (365°) oil until golden brown all over. Drain. Serve with soy sauce mixed with ginger, or mustard, or ketchup.

⟆ SERVES 3–4.

Fried Shrimp with Egg-White Batter

1 *pound raw shrimp*	*vegetable oil for deep frying*
½ *cup cornstarch*	*ketchup*
1 *teaspoon salt*	*hot mustard*
3 *egg whites*	

Shell and devein the shrimp, but leave tails on. Combine 3 tablespoons cornstarch and ½ teaspoon salt. Dip shrimp into cornstarch mixture. Beat egg whites until stiff, adding the remaining cornstarch and salt to make a batter.

Heat the oil to 365°, dip shrimp in egg-white batter and fry. Batter should remain white; do not overfry. Serve with ketchup mixed with hot mustard as a dip.

⟆ SERVES 4–6.

Fried Shrimp Balls

1 *pound shrimp, shelled,*
deveined and minced
3 *water chestnuts,*
minced
1 *teaspoon cornstarch*
1 *teaspoon salt*

½ *teaspoon minced ginger*
root or ¼ teaspoon
ground ginger
1 *teaspoon dry sherry*
1 *egg white*
vegetable oil for deep frying

Combine shrimp, water chestnuts, cornstarch, salt, ginger root or ground ginger, sherry and unbeaten egg white. Mix well and shape into small balls. Fry in hot (360°) oil until golden brown. Drain. Serve hot.

(SERVES 4–6.

Fluffy Shrimp Balls

2 *pounds raw shrimp,*
shelled and deveined
4 *water chestnuts*
¼ *pound pork fat or bacon*
4 *egg whites*
½ *teaspoon salt*

¼ *teaspoon white pepper*
½ *cup sifted flour*
2 *tablespoons ice water*
⅓ *cup cornstarch*
vegetable oil for deep frying

Combine the shrimp, water chestnuts and fat (if bacon is used, cover with water, bring to a boil, cook 2 minutes; drain) and chop together until very fine. Stir in the unbeaten egg whites, salt, pepper, flour and ice water and mix with the hand until mixture starts to turn pink. Pick up and slap down mixture on a board until it holds together. Form into walnut-size balls. Roll in the cornstarch. Fry in hot (360°) vegetable oil until balls are puffed and golden brown. Drain. Serve immediately, as the balls collapse in a few minutes.

(MAKES ABOUT 32 BALLS.

Breaded Fried Bay Scallops

1 *pound bay scallops*	¼ *teaspoon monosodium*
¼ *teaspoon salt*	*glutamate*
2 *teaspoons dry sherry*	½ *cup flour*
¼ *teaspoon ground ginger*	1 *egg, well beaten*
½ *teaspoon soy sauce*	½ *cup bread crumbs*
⅛ *teaspoon black pepper*	*vegetable oil for deep frying*

Rinse the bay scallops in cold water and dry on paper towels. Roll in a mixture of the salt, sherry, ginger, soy sauce, pepper and monosodium glutamate and place on paper towels to dry for 5 minutes. Put ½ cup flour in a paper bag, add the bay scallops a few at a time and shake to cover well. Remove from bag and shake off the excess flour. Dip the scallops first into the beaten egg and then in bread crumbs. Deep fry in hot (360°) oil until golden brown. Drain on paper towels and serve very hot.

⟅ SERVES 4.

Fried Wonton

¼ *Pound ground beef, pork,*	⅛ *teaspoon monosodium*
or chicken	*glutamate*
1 *green onion, minced*	1 *tablespoon broth or water*
¼ *teaspoon salt*	*Egg sheets for wrapping*
⅛ *teaspoon black pepper*	*(below)*
½ *teaspoon soy sauce*	1 *egg, beaten*
½ *teaspoon dry sherry*	*vegetable oil for deep frying*

Mix together the ground meat or chicken, the green onion, salt, pepper, soy sauce, sherry, monosodium glutamate and stock or water. Place 1 teaspoon of the mixture in the middle of each square. Moisten the edges of the squares with beaten egg and press the opposite corners together to form a triangle. Fry in hot (375°) oil until golden brown. Serve with Duck Sauce.

EGG SHEETS FOR WRAPPING

2 *cups sifted flour*　　　2 *eggs*
¾ *teaspoon salt*　　　　⅓ *cup cold water*

Sift together the flour and salt, place in a bowl and make a well in the center. Mix together the eggs and water and place in the well. With a wooden spoon stir until the dough will form a ball. Place the ball on a floured board and knead until stiff, adding more flour if necessary. Cover the ball of dough with a damp cloth and let stand 30 to 35 minutes. Divide into 3 pieces. Flour the board again and roll each piece into a long strip, 4 inches wide and less than ⅛-inch thick. Cut into 4-inch squares.

(MAKES ABOUT 24 WONTONS.

Cocktail Balls

1 *cup crabmeat, chopped*　　⅛ *teaspoon monosodium*
　shrimp, or any leftover　　　*glutamate*
　poultry or meat　　　　1 *egg, beaten*
1 *tablespoon minced*　　　¼ *cup dry breadcrumbs*
　onion　　　　　　　　1 *cup cooked cellophane*
¼ *teaspoon salt*　　　　　*noodles cut into ½-inch*
1 *teaspoon soy sauce*　　　*lengths*
⅛ *teaspoon black pepper*　*vegetable oil for deep frying*

Mix together the crabmeat, onion, salt, soy sauce, pepper, monosodium glutamate, egg and breadcrumbs and shape into balls the size of a walnut. Roll the balls in the noodles and fry in hot (375°) oil to a toasty brown color. They fry very quickly, in about 1 minute.

(MAKES ABOUT 24 BALLS.

Crab Cakes

1 cup crabmeat	⅛ teaspoon pepper
1 teaspoon dry sherry	½ cup seasoned mashed
½ teaspoon ground ginger	potatoes
4 tablespoons peanut or	2 eggs, beaten separately
vegetable oil	Flour for coating
2 green onions, chopped	½ cup dry breadcrumbs
½ teaspoon salt	vegetable oil for deep frying

Flake the crabmeat, sprinkle with a mixture of the sherry and ginger and set aside. Heat 4 tablespoons oil in a frying pan and sauté the green onions in it. Sprinkle with ¼ teaspoon of the salt and the pepper and remove to a large mixing bowl. Sauté the crabmeat in the same pan with the remaining ¼ teaspoon salt for 30 seconds. Add the crabmeat to the onion. Add the mashed potatoes and 1 of the beaten eggs. Mix together thoroughly and shape into cakes 1 inch in diameter and about ½-inch thick. Set aside to dry for 15 minutes, then coat with flour, and dip first into the remaining beaten egg and then in breadcrumbs. Fry in hot (375°) oil until golden brown. Serve with Chinese Mustard and Duck Sauce.

❲ MAKES 12–15 CAKES.

Soups

2

Soups

Hong Kong Corn Chowder

1 16-ounce can corn kernels,
   drained
1 tablespoon cornstarch
3 tablespoons cold water
1 egg, beaten

6 cups chicken broth
½ teaspoon white pepper
⅓ cup julienne-cut smoked
   ham or cooked chicken

Grind the corn. Mix the cornstarch and water to a smooth paste. Add to the ground corn with the egg. Bring the broth and pepper to a boil. Add the corn mixture, stirring steadily. Cover, bring again to a boil, lower heat and cook 3 minutes more. Taste for seasoning. Serve in deep bowls with the ham or chicken sprinkled on top.

(SERVES 6–8.

Corn Soup

¼ pound raw pork
1 tablespoon cornstarch
½ teaspoon sugar
¼ teaspoon black pepper
2 tablespoons soy sauce
2 tablespoons vegetable oil
1 clove garlic, minced
3 tablespoons minced
  onion
1 teaspoon minced ginger
  root or ½ teaspoon
  ground ginger

6 cups chicken
  broth
2 teaspoons salt
½ teaspoon monosodium
  glutamate
1½ cups fresh, frozen,
  or canned corn
  kernels
2 eggs, well beaten
2 green onions, thinly
  sliced

Carefully trim all fat from pork. Chop the pork and toss with the cornstarch, sugar, pepper, soy sauce and 1 tablespoon oil. Heat the remaining oil in a saucepan and sauté the garlic, onions and ginger 1 minute. Add the broth and bring to a boil. Add the salt, monosodium glutamate, corn, and pork mixture. Cover and cook over low heat 15 minutes. Combine the eggs and green onions and stir into the soup until set.

❪ SERVES 6–8.

Cabbage Soup

¼ pound raw pork
1 teaspoon cornstarch
1 teaspoon sugar
¼ teaspoon black pepper
2 tablespoons soy sauce
4 teaspoons vegetable oil
1 tablespoon sliced ginger
  root or 1 teaspoon
  ground ginger

6 cups chicken broth
2 teaspoons salt
1 head Chinese
  cabbage, coarsely
  shredded
½ teaspoon mono-
  sodium glutamate

Carefully trim all fat from pork. Cut pork into thin strips and toss with the cornstarch, sugar, pepper, soy sauce and 2 teaspoons oil. Heat the remaining oil in a saucepan and add the ginger. If using ginger root allow it to fry in the oil 2 minutes. Add the broth and salt. Bring to a boil. Add the cabbage, cover and cook over low heat 5 minutes. Stir in the pork mixture and monosodium glutamate. Cover and cook 20 minutes.

❲ SERVES 6–8.

Watercress Soup

½ *pound raw pork*
2 *teaspoons cornstarch*
½ *teaspoon sugar*
¼ *teaspoon black pepper*
2 *tablespoons soy sauce*
2 *tablespoons vegetable oil*
3 *bunches watercress*

2 *slices ginger root or* ½
  teaspoon ground ginger
6 *cups chicken broth*
2 *teaspoons salt*
½ *teaspoon monosodium*
  glutamate
2 *eggs, well beaten*

Carefully trim all fat from pork and cut meat into small dice. Toss pork with the cornstarch, sugar, pepper, soy sauce and 1 tablespoon oil. Wash and thoroughly drain watercress and discard stems. Heat the remaining oil in a saucepan and add the ginger. If using ginger root allow it to fry in the oil 1 minute. Add the broth and bring to a boil. Add the salt, monosodium glutamate, watercress and pork mixture. Cover and cook over low heat 20 minutes. Mix in the eggs, stirring until set.

❲ SERVES 6–8.

Dried Mushroom Soup

6 **Chinese dried mushrooms**
6 **cups chicken broth**
1 **cup diced bamboo shoots**

½ **cup sliced water chestnuts**
½ **cup diced celery**
2 **tablespoons soy sauce**

Wash the mushrooms and soak in warm water 10 minutes; drain and slice. Bring the broth to a boil; add the mushrooms, bamboo shoots, water chestnuts and celery. Cook over low heat 20 minutes. Mix in the soy sauce.

(SERVES 6–8.

Fresh Mushroom Soup

6 *cups chicken broth*
¼ *cup thinly sliced celery*
½ *cup chopped onion*
1 *cup sliced mushrooms*

½ *cup julienne-cut cooked chicken*
2 *tablespoons soy sauce*
2 *eggs, beaten*

Bring the broth to a boil; add the celery and onion; cook over low heat 5 minutes. Add the mushrooms and chicken; cook 5 minutes. Stir in the soy sauce, then gradually mix in the eggs until set.

(SERVES 6–8.

Tomato-Egg Soup

1 *pound tomatoes*
3 *tablespoons vegetable oil*
6 *green onions, cut in 2-inch lengths*

6 *cups beef broth*
1 *tablespoon dry sherry*
¼ *teaspoon white pepper*
1 *egg, beaten*

Peel the tomatoes and cut each into 8 wedges. Heat the oil in a saucepan; sauté the tomatoes and green onions 5 minutes. Add the broth, sherry and pepper. Bring to an active boil and slowly stir the egg into the soup. Cook until lightly set.

(SERVES 6–8.

Velvet Chicken Soup

1 small whole chicken
breast
2 egg whites
1½ teaspoons salt

2 teaspoons dry sherry
8 cups chicken broth
1 8¾-ounce can cream-style
corn

Remove the skin and bones of the chicken breast. Chop the chicken. Beat the egg whites until frothy. Mix in the chicken, salt and sherry. Bring the broth to a boil; add the chicken mixture. Bring to a boil and cook 5 minutes. Add the corn; bring to a rolling boil and serve.

(SERVES 8–10.

Chicken-Noodle Soup

1 pound fine egg
noodles
6 cups chicken broth
1 cup julienne-cut cooked
chicken

1 teaspoon sesame-seed or
corn oil
3 hard-cooked eggs,
quartered
⅓ cup chopped green onion

Cook the noodles 1 minute less than package directs. Drain and rinse under cold running water. Bring the broth to a boil; stir in the noodles, chicken and oil. Serve in deep bowls, with 2 quarters of egg in each, and a tablespoon of green onion sprinkled on top.

(SERVES 6.

Pork-Noodle Soup

Substitute 1 cup julienne-cut roast pork for the chicken.

Noodles in Broth

½ pound boneless pork
4 tablespoons vegetable oil
¼ cup thinly sliced green
   onion
½ pound spinach, washed,
   drained and shredded
3 10½-ounce cans chicken
   broth

3 cups water
2 tablespoons soy sauce
Chinese Noodles (see page
   66) or ½ pound fine
   noodles, cooked and
   drained
1 egg, beaten

Cut the pork in matchlike strips. Heat the oil in a 2- or
3-quart saucepan. Brown the pork in it. Add the green
onion and spinach; cook 3 minutes, stirring frequently.
Add the broth, water and soy sauce. Bring to a boil and
cook over low heat 5 minutes. Add the cooked, drained
noodles, bring to an active boil and slowly stir in the egg
until set.

   ❐ SERVES 6–8.

Egg-Drop Soup

½ cup minced chicken
4 water chestnuts, chopped
6 cups chicken broth

1 tablespoon cornstarch
3 tablespoons water
3 eggs, beaten

Put the chicken, water chestnuts and broth in a saucepan
and bring to a boil. Mix the cornstarch and water and add
to the soup, stirring steadily until thickened. Stir in the
eggs until set.

   ❐ SERVES 6–8.

Chicken Soup

3 or 4 pound chicken	4 green onions, chopped
2½ quarts water	1 tablespoon sherry
2 slices ginger root or ½ teaspoon ground ginger	1 tablespoon salt

Wash the chicken thoroughly. Bring the chicken and water to a boil in a deep saucepan. Add the ginger, green onions, sherry and salt. Cover and cook over low heat 2½ hours, or until chicken is very tender. Remove chicken, bone it, and cut meat into very small pieces. Strain the soup and serve with pieces of chicken meat in it.

(SERVES 8–10.

Chicken Subgum Soup

1 teaspoon vegetable oil	½ cup bean sprouts
½ cup sliced mushrooms	4 water chestnuts, diced
½ cup sliced celery	1 egg, beaten
7 cups chicken broth	2 tablespoons sliced green
1 cup diced cooked chicken	onion

Heat the oil and sauté the mushrooms and celery 1 minute. Add the chicken broth, chicken, bean sprouts and water chestnuts. Cook over medium heat 10 minutes. Mix in the beaten egg, stirring steadily. Garnish with the green onion.

(SERVES 6–8.

Chicken-Crab Soup

½ pound crabmeat	3 tablespoons cold water
6 cups chicken broth	2 eggs, beaten
1 tablespoon cornstarch	1 cup finely shredded lettuce

Pick over the crabmeat, discarding any cartilage. Bring the broth to a boil. Mix the cornstarch and water to a paste;

stir into the broth until thickened. Gradually add the eggs, stirring steadily; cook 1 minute. Mix in the crabmeat and lettuce. Bring to a boil and serve.

([SERVES 6–8.

Shrimp Soup

½ *pound raw shrimp,*
shelled and deveined
2 *egg whites, lightly*
beaten
2 *teaspoons salt*
½ *teaspoon ground ginger*
½ *cup diced celery*
1½ *cups finely shredded*
cabbage

5 *cups boiling water*
1 *10½-ounce can chicken*
broth
2 *tablespoons corn-*
starch
½ *cup chopped spinach*
¼ *cup thinly sliced green*
onion

Grind or chop the shrimp very fine. Mix in the egg whites, ½ teaspoon salt, and the ginger. Combine the celery, cabbage, water and remaining salt. Bring to a boil and cook over low heat 10 minutes. Mix the broth with the cornstarch and stir into the boiling soup until thickened Gradually add the shrimp mixture, stirring to prevent lumps from forming. Cook 5 minutes. Mix in the spinach and green onion; cook 1 minute and serve.

([SERVES 6–8.

Shrimp and Cabbage Soup

2 teaspoons vegetable oil
½ pound raw shrimp,
    shelled, deveined and
    diced
6 cups water
1 head celery cabbage or
    green cabbage, shredded
½ cup sliced water
    chestnuts
2 teaspoons
    salt
4 green onions, finely
    chopped

Heat the oil in a saucepan and sauté the shrimp 3 minutes. Add the water, cabbage, water chestnuts and salt. Bring to a boil. Cover and cook over low heat until cabbage is tender but still crisp, about 15 minutes. Sprinkle green onions on top.

◖ SERVES 4–6.

Crabmeat Soup

2 tablespoons vegetable oil
½ pound crabmeat
2 tomatoes, coarsely
    chopped
2 teaspoons chopped ginger
    root or ½ teaspoon
    ground ginger
½ teaspoon salt
5 cups chicken broth
2 eggs
2 tablespoons soy sauce
2 tablespoons vinegar
2 tablespoons dry sherry
2 green onions, thinly
    sliced

Heat the oil in a saucepan and sauté the crabmeat, tomatoes, ginger and salt 5 minutes. Add the broth. Cook over low heat 10 minutes. Beat the eggs with the soy sauce, vinegar and sherry and gradually stir into the soup. Add the green onions and cook 5 minutes.

◖ SERVES 4–6.

Fish Soup

½ pound fillet of sole
1 tablespoon dry sherry
1 tablespoon soy sauce
2 tablespoons vegetable oil
6 cups chicken broth
4 tablespoons raw rice

½ cup diced onion
½ cup diced carrot
½ cup diced celery
¼ teaspoon black pepper
4 green onions, thinly
sliced

Cut the sole into narrow slices, 1 inch long. Toss with the sherry, soy sauce and oil. Chill. Bring the broth to a boil in a saucepan. Mix in the rice, cover and cook over low heat 35 minutes. Mix in the diced onion, carrot, celery and pepper. Cover and cook 5 minutes. Stir in the sole mixture, cover and cook 10 minutes. Serve sprinkled with the green onions.

⟮ SERVES 4–6.

Shrimp and Meatball Soup

4 Chinese dried
mushrooms
½ pound ground pork
2 tablespoons chopped
green onion
1 tablespoon soy sauce
2 eggs, beaten
1 teaspoon salt
3 teaspoons cornstarch
3 teaspoons dry sherry
½ pound raw shrimp,
shelled, deveined and
chopped fine

½ teaspoon ground
ginger
8 cups beef broth
½ pound spinach, washed
and shredded
3 cups shredded
Chinese or green
cabbage
½ cup thinly sliced
bamboo shoots
1½ cups cooked fine
noodles

Soak the mushrooms in hot water for 10 minutes. Drain and slice fine. Mix together the pork, green onion, soy sauce, 1 beaten egg, ½ teaspoon salt, half the cornstarch and half the sherry. Form into marble-sized balls. Mix together the shrimp, ginger and the remaining egg, salt, cornstarch and sherry. Shape into marble-sized balls.

Bring the broth to a boil; add the mushrooms, spinach, cabbage, bamboo shoots and shrimp and pork balls. Cook over low heat 25 minutes. Stir in the noodles and taste for seasoning.

(SERVES 8–10.

Meatball Soup

½ *pound raw pork*   ½ *teaspoon salt*
¼ *cup finely chopped green*   ¼ *teaspoon black pepper*
  onion   2 *egg yolks*
2 *teaspoons soy sauce*   6 *cups chicken broth*

Chop the pork very fine. Add the green onion, soy sauce, salt, pepper and egg yolks and mix thoroughly. Shape into ½-inch balls. Bring the broth to a boil and carefully drop in the meatballs. Cover and cook over low heat 45 minutes.

(SERVES 6–8.

Meatball and Vermicelli Soup

¼ *pound fine noodles or*   ¼ *teaspoon black pepper*
  vermicelli, broken into   4 *tablespoons vegetable oil*
  2-inch pieces   6 *cups beef broth*
2 *tablespoons cornstarch*   3 *green onions, cut in*
¼ *cup water*   *½-inch pieces*
½ *pound ground pork*   2 *tablespoons soy sauce*
1 *teaspoon salt*

Cover the noodles with boiling water and soak 5 minutes. Drain thoroughly. Blend the cornstarch and water. Mix into the ground pork with the salt and pepper. Form into

walnut-size balls. Heat the oil in a skillet and fry meatballs until brown all over. Bring the broth to a boil in a
saucepan and cook the noodles 5 minutes. Carefully add
the meatballs and cook 5 minutes. Mix in the green onions
and soy sauce. Cook 3 minutes.

〖 SERVES 6–8.

Wonton Soup

¼ pound ground pork or
  equal quantities of
  ground shrimp and
  pork
1 green onion, minced
¼ teaspoon salt
1 teaspoon soy
  sauce
⅛ teaspoon pepper
⅛ teaspoon monosodium
  glutamate
1 egg
1½ teaspoons cold water

Egg sheets for wrapping
  (see page 32 under Fried
  Wonton in Appetizer
  section), each cut into
  4 squares
¼ cup cold water mixed
  with ½ tablespoon
  cornstarch
3 cups chicken broth
½ cup shredded Chinese
  cabbage
Julienne strips of boiled ham,
  optional

Mix together the ground pork (or shrimp and pork),
onion, salt, soy sauce, pepper, monosodium glutamate, egg
and 1½ teaspoons cold water. Place ½ teaspoon of the
mixture on each square of the egg sheets (you will have
24 squares). Moisten the edges with the water and cornstarch mixture. Fold over, bringing the opposite corners
together to form a triangle. Press to seal. Drop the wontons
into boiling water; allow water to come to a boil again,
add 2 cups cold water, cover and bring to a boil once
more. Remove wontons, rinse quickly in cold water and
drain. Bring the chicken broth to a boil, add the Chinese

cabbage and cook 3 minutes. Add the wontons and bring to a boil again. Garnish with ham strips, if desired.

❐ MAKES 24 WONTONS; SERVES 4.

Bean-Curd Soup

5 cups beef or chicken
broth
1 cup shredded Chinese
cabbage
3 water chestnuts, thinly
sliced
¼ cup bamboo shoots
¼ pound thinly sliced pork
¼ teaspoon salt
½ teaspoon soy sauce

⅛ teaspoon black pepper
⅛ teaspoon monosodium
glutamate
1 teaspoon peanut or
vegetable oil
2 cakes bean-curd, each
cut into 6 pieces
4 snow-pea pods, each cut
in half

Bring the broth to a boil and add the cabbage, water chestnuts and bamboo shoots. Cover and bring again to a boil, then simmer 3 minutes. Add the slices of pork, which have been seasoned with a mixture of the salt, soy sauce, pepper, monosodium glutamate and oil. Then add the bean-curd and the snow-pea pods and bring once again to a boil. Simmer 2 minutes and serve very hot.

❐ SERVES 4–5.

Chinese Okra Soup

¾ pound lean pork
6 cups water
½ cup diced raw shrimp
1 tablespoon crushed
fresh ginger or
1 teaspoon powdered

1 pound okra,
sliced
½ cup chopped green
onion
½ teaspoon salt

Bring the pork and water to a boil. Add ginger and simmer 20 minutes. Add shrimp and okra and simmer 10 minutes more. Remove the pork and slice thin. Add the slices to the soup and reheat. Add the chopped green onion and the salt and serve very hot.

(SERVES 4–5.

Oxtail Soup

1 *oxtail, cut in 2-inch pieces*	2 *tablespoons soy sauce*
¼ *cup black beans*	1 *teaspoon salt*
½ *cup raw peanuts, in the shell*	1 *onion, sliced*
	2 *cups sliced carrots*
2 *tablespoons peanut or vegetable oil*	2 *cups sliced turnips*
	8 *cups water*

Wash oxtail and remove excess fat. Wash beans and soak 2 hours in 1 cup water. Wash peanuts and soak 2 hours in water to cover. Drain peanuts, add fresh water to cover, bring to a boil and boil 5 minutes. Drain and shell. Bring oxtail to a boil in 3 cups water, then simmer 5 minutes, and drain. In a skillet heat 2 tablespoons oil and sauté oxtail 2 minutes, stirring to brown all sides. Add soy sauce and salt. Combine oxtail, beans, peanuts, onion, carrots and turnips. Add 8 cups water, bring to a boil, then simmer 2 hours. Remove oxtail and separate meat from bones. Return meat to soup and reheat.

(SERVES 6.

Hot-and-Sour Soup

4 *Chinese mushrooms*
1 *cup water*
¼ *pound lean pork or*
   1 *chicken breast*
2 *tablespoons vegetable oil*
4 *cups beef or chicken*
   broth
2 *tablespoons cornstarch*
2 *tablespoons dry sherry*
2 *tablespoons white vinegar*

2 *bean-curd cakes*
1 *teaspoon salt*
1 *teaspoon soy sauce*
⅛ *teaspoon dried ground*
   red peppers
1 *egg, beaten*
1 *tablespoon sesame-seed*
   oil
1 *green onion, thinly sliced*

Wash the mushrooms and soak in the water for 30 minutes. Drain, reserving the water; cut the mushrooms into matchlike strips. Cut the pork or chicken into narrow strips. Heat the vegetable oil in a saucepan and cook the pork or chicken in it for 5 minutes. Add the broth, mushrooms, mushroom water; bring to a boil and cook over low heat 10 minutes. Mix together the cornstarch, sherry and vinegar; stir into the soup until thickened. Add the bean-curd, salt, soy sauce and red pepper. Stir in the egg, then the sesame-seed oil and green onion. Taste for seasoning; the soup should be a little tart and spicy. Add more vinegar and red pepper if necessary.

《 SERVES 4–6.

Eggs

3

Eggs

Scrambled Eggs with Pork

⅓ cup vegetable oil
½ pound ground pork
¼ cup thinly sliced green
  onion

6 eggs, beaten
¼ cup soy sauce
1 tablespoon dry sherry
½ teaspoon sugar

Heat the oil in a skillet; add the pork and green onion.
Cook over medium heat, stirring almost constantly, until
pork is brown. Remove the pork and onions. Scramble the
eggs in the oil remaining in the skillet until they begin to
set. Return the pork mixture and add the soy sauce, sherry
and sugar. Cook, stirring steadily, for a few seconds.
⟮ SERVES 4–6.

Egg Fu Yung

¾ cup peanut or
  vegetable oil
1 green onion, chopped
½ cup cooked pork, ham,
  chicken or shellfish
1 tablespoon soy sauce

1 teaspoon salt
1 cup bean sprouts
¼ cup sliced mushrooms,
  canned or fresh
4 eggs, beaten
Sauce (see page 56)

Heat 2 tablespoons oil in a skillet until very hot. Add the chopped onion and stir 2 minutes. Remove pan from heat and add the cooked meat, chicken or shellfish, the soy sauce, salt, bean sprouts and mushrooms. Mix well, drain and allow to cool. When completely cooled, stir in the beaten eggs. Have oil for frying ½-inch deep in a skillet and bring to 375°. With a soup ladle, spoon the meat and vegetable mixture into the oil, frying about ¼ of the mixture at a time. Allow to get golden brown on both sides, then serve immediately with sauce.

SAUCE

1 *cup water*
1 *teaspoon soy sauce*
2 *tablespoons oyster sauce*
⅛ *teaspoon monosodium glutamate*
¼ *teaspoon salt*
2 *tablespoons cornstarch mixed with 2 tablespoons cold water*
⅛ *teaspoon black pepper*

Bring the water to a boil. Add the other ingredients with the exception of the cornstarch paste. Remove from heat, thicken with the paste, return to heat and simmer 2 minutes.

If desired, the Fu Yung may be garnished with additional chopped green onion.

◖ SERVES 6.

Vegetable Omelet

oons vegetable oil ½ cup chopped mushrooms
opped onion 1 teaspoon salt
nely chopped green ¼ teaspoon black pepper
rs 6 eggs
nely chopped celery 2 teaspoons soy sauce

tablespoons oil in a skillet; sauté the onion 5
Add the green peppers, celery, mushrooms, salt
per; sauté 5 minutes. Cool for 10 minutes. Beat
with the soy sauce. Stir in the vegetables. Heat
ining oil in the skillet; pour the egg mixture into
over low heat until browned and firm, lifting the
allow uncooked mixture to run under. Cut into
ed wedges.

ves 4–6.

Chinese Fried Eggs

blespoons peanut or ¼ cup bamboo
getable oil shoots
ove garlic, crushed 3 Chinese dried mush-
p shredded cooked rooms, soaked in warm
ork water 30 minutes, drained
aspoon salt and shredded
easpoons soy sauce ½ cup water
easpoon black pepper ½ cup bean sprouts
easpoon monosodium 1 teaspoon cornstarch
lutamate mixed with 2 teaspoons
hin slices ginger root cold water
r ½ teaspoon ground 4 eggs
inger

Special Egg Fu Yung

2 Chinese dried mushrooms 1 tablespoon water
½ cup vegetable oil ½ pound crabmeat, picked
2 bamboo shoots, chopped over and flaked
2 green onions, thinly 1 teaspoon minced ginger
sliced root or ½ teaspoon
½ cup canned green peas ground ginger
2 tablespoons soy sauce 1 tablespoon dry sherry
1 cup chicken broth 6 eggs
1 tablespoon cornstarch 1½ teaspoons salt

Wash the mushrooms, cover with warm water and let soak
15 minutes. Drain and chop. Heat 2 tablespoons oil in a
skillet and sauté the bamboo shoots, mushrooms and green
onions 3 minutes. Mix in green peas, soy sauce and broth.
When liquid boils, add cornstarch mixed with water, stirring until thickened. Mix the crabmeat with the ginger
root and sherry. Lightly beat the eggs and mix in the
crabmeat mixture and salt. Heat the remaining oil in a
11-inch omelet pan or skillet, add egg mixture and cook
until set. (Can also be cooked as 5 or 6 individual pancakes.) Turn over and brown on second side. Turn out
onto a heated dish and pour sauce over it.

serves 4–6.

Note: Chopped shrimp, chicken or roast pork can be
substituted for crab.

Crab Fu Yung

1 cup crabmeat, flaked 2 tablespoons cornstarch
1 tablespoon dry sherry 1 cup milk
½ teaspoon ground ginger ½ cup vegetable oil
4 egg whites 1 tablespoon chopped
¼ teaspoon salt parsley

Remove any shell from crabmeat. Combine with sherry and ginger. Beat the egg whites stiff and mix in the salt and cornstarch. Mix in the crabmeat and milk. Heat the oil in an 11-inch skillet. Pour the crabmeat mixture into it. Cook, stirring steadily, until thickened. Turn out onto a hot plate and sprinkle top with parsley.

(SERVES 3–4.

Chicken Fu Yung

1 *whole raw chicken breast*	½ *pound snow peas*
6 *tablespoons water*	8 *small slices bamboo*
1 *teaspoon dry sherry*	*shoot*
1 *teaspoon salt*	1 *cup chicken*
2 *tablespoons cornstarch*	*broth*
6 *egg whites, beaten stiff*	¼ *teaspoon monosodium*
⅔ *cup plus 2 tablespoons*	*glutamate*
vegetable oil	

Remove the skin and bones and grind the chicken. Add 3 tablespoons water to the ground chicken, a few drops at a time, mixing well. Mix in the sherry, ½ teaspoon salt and 1 tablespoon cornstarch. Gradually fold in the egg whites. Heat ⅔ cup oil in a skillet and add chicken mixture. Immediately remove from heat and stir briskly. Return to heat and cook until firm but not brown. (Result will be like an omelet.)

Heat the remaining 2 tablespoons oil in another skillet and sauté the snow peas and bamboo shoots 2 minutes. Mix in the chicken broth. Bring to a boil. Combine the monosodium glutamate with the remaining salt, cornstarch and water and stir into pan until thickened. Put omelet in a dish and cover with vegetables and sauce.

(SERVES 2–4.

E[g...]

½ *pound shrimp, shel[...]*
  deveined and diced[...]
1 *teaspoon dry sherry[...]*
½ *teaspoon ground gin[...]*

Toss shrimp with the s[...]
3 tablespoons oil in a s[...]
turn pink. Drain and co[...]

Lightly beat the eggs [...]
salt. Heat the remaining [...]
bubbles. Add the shrimp [...]
brown on underside. Tu[...]
second side.

(SERVES 4–6.

Chine[...]

1 *tablespoon cornstarch*
1 *cup chicken broth*
1½ *tablespoons soy sauce*
1 *teaspoon sugar*
2 *eggs*
½ *teaspoon salt*

Mix the cornstarch with the [...]
Cook over low heat, stirring s[...]
over very low heat while prep[...]

Beat the eggs, salt and wa[...]
chicken or shrimp, and the g[...]
skillets or one 11-inch skillet. F[...]
Divide the mixture between th[...]
in the large pan. Fry until brow[...]
to hot plates and pour the sauc[...]

(SERVES 2.

½ *cup c[...]*
½ *cup fi[...]*
  peppe[...]
½ *cup fi[...]*

Heat 2 [...]
minutes.[...]
and pep[...]
the eggs [...]
the rem[...]
it. Cook[...]
edges to [...]
pie-shap[...]

(SER[...]

6 *ta[...]*
  ve[...]
1 *cl[...]*
½ *cu[...]*
  p[...]
½ *to[...]*
2½ *to[...]*
⅛ *to[...]*
¼ *to[...]*
  g[...]
2 *t[...]*

Heat 3 tablespoons oil in a frying pan and brown the garlic in it. Season the pork with ¼ teaspoon salt, ½ teaspoon soy sauce, pepper, and monosodium glutamate, and cook with the garlic 1 minute. Remove the mixture from the pan. In the same pan heat 1 tablespoon oil, add the ginger, the remaining ¼ teaspoon salt, bamboo shoots and mushrooms and stir 2 minutes. Add ½ cup water, cover, and cook 2 minutes. Add the bean sprouts and stir 1 minute longer. Add the pork and the remaining 2 teaspoons soy sauce, and thicken with the cornstarch paste. In another frying pan fry the eggs in 2 tablespoons hot oil on one side only. Place the pork mixture in a serving dish and garnish with the fried eggs.

(SERVES 4.

Eggs in Sweet-and-Sour Sauce

3 tablespoons peanut or vegetable oil	¼ cup shredded carrot
¼ teaspoon salt	4 eggs
¼ cup diced cucumber, unpeeled but seeded	Sauce (see below)
	chopped parsley

Heat 1 tablespoon oil in a frying pan. Add the salt, cucumber and carrot and cook 1 minute, stirring constantly. In another frying pan heat the remaining 2 tablespoons oil. Break 1 egg into the pan, reduce heat to low, and when the white has congealed below but the upper surface is still moist, flip one half of the egg over the other to form a semicircle. Press with a spatula to seal the halves together. Cook to a golden color on both sides. Place egg in serving dish and repeat procedure with the remaining 3 eggs. Arrange the eggs on a platter and cover with the vegetables. Pour the sauce on top and garnish with parsley.

SAUCE

1 *cup water*

2 *slices ginger root or ½ teaspoon ground ginger*

¼ *cup sugar*

¼ *cup cider vinegar*

½ *teaspoon salt*

1 *tablespoon soy sauce*

1 *teaspoon chopped sweet gherkins*

2 *teaspoons cornstarch mixed with 1 tablespoon cold water*

Bring the water to a boil; add the remaining ingredients with the exception of the cornstarch paste. Cook 2 minutes, remove the slices of ginger, thicken with the paste and cook 1 minute longer.

❲ SERVES 4.

Ham and Eggs, Chinese Style

4 *strips bacon, cut into ½-inch pieces*

½ *cup cooked peas*

1 *green onion, chopped*

½ *teaspoon salt*

⅛ *teaspoon black pepper*

¼ *cup diced cooked ham*

4 *eggs, beaten*

⅛ *teaspoon monosodium glutamate*

2 *tablespoons peanut or vegetable oil*

In a hot skillet lightly brown the bacon and add the peas, green onion, salt and pepper. When well mixed, add the ham and set aside. Beat the eggs and add the monosodium glutamate, then combine with the ham mixture. In another frying pan heat 2 tablespoons oil, add the egg mixture and remove the pan from the heat. Stir, and when the mixture begins to set, remove to a hot serving dish. On the way to the table the hot serving dish will complete the cooking of the eggs.

❲ SERVES 2–4.

Rice, Noodles and Dumplings

4

Rice, Noodles and Dumplings

Boiled Rice

1 *cup raw long-grain rice*   1 *teaspoon salt*
1½ *cups cold water*

Wash the rice under cold running water until water runs clear. Combine in a deep saucepan with the water and salt. (The Chinese don't use salt, so omit it if you prefer.) Cover, bring to a boil and cook over high heat 15 minutes or until dry and tender. Don't stir.

(MAKES 2 CUPS.

Fried Rice

4 *cups cooked drained rice*
4 *tablespoons vegetable oil*
¾ *cup chopped green onion*
1½ *cups julienne-cut cooked chicken or roast pork*

1 *teaspoon salt*
¼ *teaspoon black pepper*
2 *eggs, beaten*
2 *tablespoons soy sauce*
½ *cup finely chopped parsley*

The rice should be cooked a day ahead (see page 65) and refrigerated overnight. Heat the oil in a deep skillet, add the cold rice and cook until lightly browned, stirring constantly and pressing out any lumps. Mix in the green onion, chicken or pork, salt and pepper, and cook 1 minute, stirring constantly. Make a hollow in the center and pour in the eggs. Stir the eggs in the "rice bowl" until they begin to set, then mix them into the rice. Mix in the soy sauce and parsley.

❲ SERVES 4–6.

Note: Cooked ham, lobster, shrimp, or bean sprouts may be substituted for the pork or chicken.

Chinese Noodles

2 *cups flour*	1 *cup water*
¼ *teaspoon salt*	

Mix the flour, salt and water until a dough is formed. Turn out onto a floured surface and knead until smooth and elastic. Cover with a damp cloth and let stand 30 minutes. Knead again, then roll out and stretch very thin. Fold over into 5 layers and slice very thin. Shake to separate, and let dry for 30 minutes. Cook in 2 quarts boiling water 7 minutes, or until tender. Drain. Use as directed in recipes.

❲ MAKES ½ POUND.

Egg Noodles

4 *cups flour*	2 *eggs*
1 *teaspoon salt*	*water*

Sift the flour and salt into a bowl. Work in the eggs and just enough water to make a stiff dough. Turn out onto a lightly floured surface and knead until smooth and

elastic. Cover with a bowl and leave 10 minutes. Place
dough on floured board and roll out, using a forward
motion, away from you. Fold over and roll out again as
thin as possible. Roll up like a jelly-roll. Cut into very fine
strips, sprinkle lightly with flour, and toss gently to separate. Cook noodles in boiling salted water for 8 minutes.
Drain well and serve, or use as directed in other recipes.

❨ MAKES 1 POUND.

Fried Noodles with Shrimp

6 *Chinese dried
mushrooms*
½ *pound raw shrimp,
shelled, deveined and
diced*
1 *teaspoon minced ginger
root or ½ teaspoon
ground ginger*
2 *tablespoons soy sauce*
1 *tablespoon sherry*

1 *tablespoon cornstarch*
5 *tablespoons
vegetable oil*
1 *cup shredded cabbage*
1 *cup sliced bamboo
shoots*
1½ *teaspoons salt*
3 *cups cooked and chilled
fine noodles*

Soak the mushrooms in hot water 20 minutes. Drain well
and slice. Mix the shrimp, ginger, soy sauce, sherry and
cornstarch. Heat 2 tablespoons oil in a skillet. Add the
cabbage, bamboo shoots, mushrooms and salt, and cook
5 minutes, stirring frequently. Remove. Add 1 tablespoon
oil to skillet and heat. Add shrimp mixture and sauté
3 minutes. Mix in cooked vegetables and cook 1 minute.
Heat the remaining oil in another skillet and fry the
noodles 5 minutes, turning frequently. Stir in the shrimp-
vegetable mixture and cook 2 minutes more over high
heat, stirring constantly.

❨ SERVES 4–6.

Fried Noodles with Pork

½ pound boneless pork

4 eggs

2 teaspoons salt

¾ cup vegetable oil

½ pound mushrooms, sliced

½ cup sliced green onion

½ cup sliced water
chestnuts

2 tablespoons soy sauce

2 tablespoons dry sherry

1 teaspoon monosodium
glutamate

Chinese noodles (page 66) or
½ pound of any fine
noodles, cooked, drained,
and chilled

Cut the pork in matchlike pieces. Beat the eggs with ½ teaspoon salt. Heat 2 tablespoons of the oil in a 9-inch skillet. Pour in the eggs and cook until set and browned on both sides. Turn out onto a plate and cut in narrow strips. Heat 3 tablespoons oil in the skillet; brown the pork in it. Add the mushrooms, green onion and water chestnuts. Cook over medium heat 5 minutes, stirring frequently. Mix in the soy sauce, sherry and monosodium glutamate. Keep hot while preparing the noodles. Heat the remaining oil in a skillet. Add the cooked noodles and remaining salt. Cook over high heat, stirring almost constantly, until browned, about 5 minutes. Heap in a bowl, cover with the pork mixture, and sprinkle the egg strips over all.

(SERVES 2–4.

Fried Noodles with Vegetables

10 *Chinese dried mushrooms*
½ *cup hot water*
4 *tablespoons*
  vegetable oil
1 *cup sliced celery*
1 *cup sliced bamboo shoots*
1 *pound fresh spinach or*
  1 *package frozen, thawed*

1 *teaspoon salt*
3 *cups cooked, drained*
  noodles
3 *tablespoons soy sauce*
2 *teaspoons cornstarch*
3 *tablespoons sliced green*
  onion

Wash the mushrooms. Put in a bowl with the hot water
and soak 30 minutes. Drain and slice mushrooms, reserving water. Heat the oil in a deep skillet and sauté the
celery, mushrooms and bamboo shoots 3 minutes. Add
the spinach and salt and cook 1 minute, stirring constantly.
Mix in the noodles and cook 3 minutes, stirring frequently.
Mix the soy sauce, cornstarch and reserved water from
mushrooms. Stir into the skillet until mixture is thickened.
Serve sprinkled with the green onion.

⟪ SERVES 4–6.

Boiled Wonton

DOUGH

2 *cups sifted flour*
1 *teaspoon salt*

2 *eggs*
⅓ *cup water*

Sift the flour and salt into a bowl. Beat the egg and stir
in. Add the water gradually, mixing lightly until a dough
is formed. You may not need to add all the water. Turn
onto a lightly floured surface and knead until very smooth.
Cover with a bowl and leave 30 minutes. Roll out as thin
as possible. Cut into 3-inch squares. Put a tablespoon of
desired filling in the center of each square. Fold over to

form a triangle, pressing edges together to seal. Cook in boiling salted water, or in clear soup, for 15 minutes.

❡ MAKES ABOUT 24.

FISH FILLING

½ *pound raw cleaned*
shrimp or fish, finely
chopped
2 *green onions, finely*
chopped
3 *tablespoons minced*
parsley
1 *teaspoon minced ginger*
root or ½ teaspoon
ground ginger

1 *egg, beaten*
1 *tablespoon*
vegetable oil
1 *tablespoon soy sauce*
1 *teaspoon corn-*
starch
½ *teaspoon sugar*
½ *teaspoon salt*
¼ *teaspoon black pepper*

Combine all the ingredients, mixing well. Use as directed.

MEAT FILLING

½ *pound finely ground*
raw pork or chicken
3 *water chestnuts, finely*
chopped
2 *green onions, finely*
chopped

1 *egg, beaten*
1 *tablespoon soy sauce*
½ *teaspoon salt*
¼ *teaspoon black*
pepper

Combine all the ingredients, mixing well. Use as directed.

Fried Beef Dumplings

DOUGH

1 *cup flour*   ½ *cup boiling water*

Mix the flour and boiling water until a dough is formed. If too dry, add a little more boiling water; if too sticky, a little more flour. Form into a ball, cover with a damp cloth and let stand 30 minutes. Prepare the filling meanwhile.

FILLING

4 *tablespoons vegetable oil*	¼ *teaspoon salt*
¼ *pound ground beef*	½ *teaspoon ground ginger*
¼ *cup chopped green onion*	2 *tablespoons dry sherry*
1 *tablespoon soy sauce*	1 *cup water*

Heat 2 tablespoons oil in a skillet; brown the meat in it. Remove from the heat and stir in the green onion, soy sauce, salt, ginger and sherry. Cool.

Knead the dough on a floured surface until elastic. Form into a long roll about ¾ inch in diameter. Cut into 1-inch lengths, flatten with the hand, and roll out each piece into 3-inch circles. Sprinkle with flour to facilitate rolling. The dough should be very thin at this point. Place 2 teaspoons of filling on each circle and fold over into a half moon, sealing the edges by moistening with a little water and pinching them together.

Use two 8-inch skillets; heat 1 tablespoon of oil in each. Arrange the dumplings in rows in skillets, being sure the edges touch. Fry until dumplings are browned on the bottom. Add ½ cup water to each skillet. Cover and cook over low heat until the water is absorbed. Turn out browned side up. The dumplings should be stuck together. Serve hot with Chinese mustard.

❨ MAKES ABOUT 16.

Steamed Beef Dumplings

1 *pound lean ground beef*
2 *green onions, minced*
½ *teaspoon salt*
2 *teaspoons soy sauce*
⅛ *teaspoon pepper*
¼ *teaspoon monosodium glutamate*
1 *teaspoon cornstarch*
½ *teaspoon powdered ginger*
1 *tablespoon sherry*
5 *tablespoons stock or water*
¼ *cup cooked peas, optional*
8 *egg sheets for wrapping (see page 32) each cut in 4 squares*
beaten egg mixed with 1 tablespoon water

Mix together all the ingredients except the egg sheets. Place 1 tablespoon of the mixture on each egg-sheet square. Moisten the edges of the dough with the egg-water mixture. Bring the opposite corners of the square together to form a triangle. Press the edges to seal. Arrange the dumplings in a cake pan and steam 8 minutes. Serve hot with Chinese mustard and Duck Sauce.

❪ MAKES ABOUT 32 DUMPLINGS.

Fried Pork Dumplings

FILLING

1 *pound ground pork*
2 *green onions, minced*
1 *tablespoon sherry*
½ *teaspoon ground ginger*
½ *teaspoon salt*
1 *tablespoon soy sauce*
¼ *teaspoon cornstarch*
2 *cups Chinese celery cabbage shredded, parboiled and drained*

Mix the above ingredients together thoroughly and enclose (1 heaping teaspoon to each round of dough) in wrappings made as follows:

WRAPPINGS

2 *cups sifted flour*   1 *teaspoon salt*
1 *cup boiling water*

Sift the flour and salt into a bowl. Stir in the boiling water to make a dough. Knead on a floured board until smooth. Shape into walnut-size balls, coat each ball with flour, and roll out into thin 2½-inch rounds. Put 1 heaping teaspoon of filling into the center of each round; fold over to make a semicircle. Press the opposite edges together firmly. Pan fry in 2 tablespoons hot oil 1 minute, add ½ cup water, cover, and simmer slowly 5 minutes. Uncover, raise heat to medium high and cook until water is evaporated. Add 2 more tablespoons oil and continue to cook until brown on one side. Serve hot with soy sauce.

(MAKES ABOUT 32 DUMPLINGS.

Chinese Bread

½ *envelope yeast*   2 *cups sifted flour*
½ *teaspoon sugar*   ½ *teaspoon salt*
½ *cup warm water*

Sprinkle the yeast and sugar into the water. Let stand 5 minutes, then mix until dissolved. Mix with the flour and salt until a dough is formed. If too dry, add a little more warm water. Knead until smooth and elastic. Place dough in an oiled bowl, cover and let rise 4 hours.

Divide dough into 18 pieces. Roll out each piece into a thin circle; then fold over into a half moon, but don't seal edges. Place a piece of parchment paper or aluminum foil under each, then arrange on a greased rack. Place the rack in a pan and add boiling water to just below the rack. Cover the pan and cook over low heat 30 minutes.

Serve with crisp Soy Chicken, Szechwan Duck or any Chinese dish.

Fish and Seafood

5

Fish and Seafood

Crisp-Fried Fish

1½ pounds smelts or
   2 1-pound whole fish
   (sole, trout, snapper)
½ tablespoon dry sherry
½ cup soy sauce
  6 slices ginger root or 1
   teaspoon ground ginger

½ teaspoon anise
vegetable oil for deep
   frying
1 tablespoon sesame-
   seed oil or vege-
   table oil

Have the whole fish cleaned, heads and tails removed, if you like. (The Chinese leave them on.) Wash and dry. Combine the sherry, soy sauce, ginger root or ground ginger and anise. Marinate the fish in the mixture 30 minutes, basting and turning frequently. Drain and wipe dry. Heat the oil to 365° and fry fish until crisp and browned. Drain. Serve cold, sprinkled with sesame-seed oil.

❲ SERVES 4–6.

Fish Rolls

4 *fillets of sole*	½ *teaspoon ground ginger*
1 *egg, beaten*	¼ *cup finely chopped green*
1 *tablespoon soy sauce*	*onion*
1 *tablespoon cornstarch*	½ *cup ground peanuts*
1½ *teaspoons salt*	4 *slices ham*
1½ *teaspoons sugar*	2 *cups vegetable oil*

Cut the fillets in half crosswise; wash and dry. Dip in a mixture of the egg, soy sauce, cornstarch, salt, sugar, and ginger. Sprinkle 1 side with some of the green onion and the peanuts and over it place a half slice of ham cut to fit the fish. Roll up the fish and tie with thread or fasten with toothpicks.

Heat the oil in a deep skillet until it bubbles. Fry the rolls in it until browned on all sides. Drain and serve hot.

❲ SERVES 4–8.

Batter-Fried Fish-Spinach Rolls

1 *pound fish fillets*	1 *cup flour*
1 *teaspoon salt*	1 *egg*
½ *teaspoon ground ginger*	⅔ *cup water*
¼ *cup minced ham*	2 *tablespoons sesame seeds*
1 *cup shredded raw spinach*	*vegetable oil for deep frying*

Cut the fish fillets into pieces 4 inches long and 1½ inches wide. Sprinkle with the salt and ginger. Put some ham and spinach on each piece of fish, roll up and fasten with toothpicks. Make a batter of the flour, eggs and water. Stir in the sesame seeds. Dip the fish rolls in the batter, coating them well. Heat the oil to 365°. Fry the rolls in it until browned. Don't crowd the pan. Drain.

❲ SERVES 4–6.

Fish in Brown Sauce

2 pounds fish (sea bass, carp, pike)	3 tablespoons dry sherry
	1 tablespoon soy sauce
⅓ cup flour	½ cup beef broth
½ cup vegetable oil	½ teaspoon sugar
½ cup sliced green onion	¼ teaspoon cinnamon
1 clove garlic, minced	¼ teaspoon anise
¾ cup sliced mushrooms	

Wash and dry the fish and cut into ½-inch slices. Dip lightly in the flour. Heat the oil in a skillet; brown the fish in it on both sides. Pour off all but 2 tablespoons oil. Add the green onion, garlic and mushrooms; cook 1 minute, stirring constantly. Add the sherry, soy sauce, broth, sugar, cinnamon and anise. Bring to a boil, cover and cook over low heat 15 minutes. Baste frequently.

(SERVES 6.

Pork-Stuffed Fish

3 pound bass or carp	1 tablespoon dry sherry
2½ teaspoons salt	⅓ cup vegetable oil
½ teaspoon black pepper	2 cups water
¼ pound ground pork	1 tablespoon sugar
½ cup minced green onion	1 clove garlic, minced
1 teaspoon ground ginger	3 tablespoons julienne-cut
4 tablespoons soy sauce	preserved ginger

Have the fish cleaned, split, and bone removed. The head may be removed or not, as you prefer. Rub the fish with 2 teaspoons of the salt and the pepper. Cut 3 crosswise slashes on each side. Mix together the pork, ¼ cup green onion, the ground ginger, 1 tablespoon soy sauce, the sherry and remaining salt. Stuff the fish and sew or skewer the opening.

Heat the oil in a skillet large enough to hold the fish. Brown fish on both sides. Mix together in a saucepan the water, sugar, garlic, preserved ginger and the remaining soy sauce and green onion. Bring to a boil. Drain the oil from the fish and add the sauce. Cook over low heat 40 minutes, turning the fish once.

(SERVES 4–6.

Stuffed Fish

3 *pound bass, carp or red snapper*
6 *Chinese dried shrimp or ½ cup cooked chopped shrimp*
6 *Chinese dried mushrooms or ⅓ cup chopped fresh mushrooms*
¼ *cup minced green onion*
6 *water chestnuts, diced*
⅛ *pound diced smoked ham*
1 *tablespoon minced parsley*
1 *teaspoon salt*
¼ *teaspoon black pepper*
2 *tablespoons ice water*
1 *cup vegetable oil*
½ *cup cornstarch*
2 *tablespoons dry sherry*
1 *tablespoon sugar*
1 *tablespoon soy sauce*
2 *teaspoons minced ginger root or 1 teaspoon ground ginger*
½ *cup warm water*

Have the fish split and boned, and the head removed. With a very sharp knife carefully scrape the flesh away from the skin, without tearing the skin. Spread the skin out on a flat surface. Chop the flesh very fine. If dried shrimp and mushrooms are used, soak them separately in lukewarm water for 30 minutes; thoroughly drain and chop. Combine the chopped fish, shrimp, mushrooms, green onion, water chestnuts, ham, parsley, salt, pepper, ice water, 1 tablespoon oil and 1 tablespoon cornstarch, mixing well. Spread on half the fish skin and cover with other side of skin. Press edges together. Secure with toothpicks, if necessary. Heat remaining oil in a skillet. Coat fish with remaining cornstarch and brown in hot oil on both sides. Drain off the oil. Combine the sherry, sugar, soy sauce, ginger root and warm water and pour over the fish. Cover and cook over low heat 20 minutes, turning fish once.

⟨ SERVES 6.

Fried Fluffy Fish Balls

1 *pound white-meat fish fillets (flounder, sole or cod)*
2 *cups water*
2 *egg whites*
3 *tablespoons cornstarch*
2 *teaspoons dry sherry*
1 *teaspoon salt*
½ *teaspoon ground ginger*
¼ *teaspoon monosodium glutamate*
vegetable oil for deep frying
2 *tablespoons soy sauce*
1 *tablespoon cider vinegar*
1 *tablespoon sugar*

Put the fish through a meat grinder, gradually adding 1 cup water while grinding—or blend in an electric blender. Beat the egg whites until stiff, gradually adding 2 tablespoons of the cornstarch. Combine with ground fish, sherry, salt, ginger and monosodium glutamate. Mix thoroughly. Form teaspoons of the mixture into balls. Heat the oil to 370°. Fry the balls until browned. Drain. Mix the remaining cornstarch with the remaining water. Heat the soy sauce, vinegar and sugar and stir in cornstarch mixture until thickened. Serve fish balls and sauce in separate bowls.

Steamed Fish with Sweet-Sour Sauce

2 whole 1½-pound pike or other white-meat fish	4 thin slices ginger root
3 tablespoons dry sherry	1 tablespoon chopped cucumber pickle
1½ teaspoons salt	2 tablespoons cider vinegar seeded and cut in small pieces
½ teaspoon ground ginger	
4 tablespoons vegetable oil	2 tablespoons sugar
2 sweet red peppers,	1 tablespoon soy sauce
1 small green pepper, seeded and diced	2 teaspoons cornstarch
	1 cup water

Wash and dry the fish and slash each side three times, crosswise. Arrange on a baking dish and sprinkle with the sherry, salt and ginger. Put dish on a rack in a saucepan. Add boiling water to reach rack. Cover the saucepan and cook over low heat 30 minutes, or until fish flakes easily when tested with a fork.

Heat 2 tablespoons oil in a skillet and sauté the green and red pepper, ginger and cucumber pickle 3 minutes. Stir in the vinegar, sugar, soy sauce and remaining oil. Mix the cornstarch and water and stir into pepper mixture until thickened. Pour sauce over fish and serve.

◖ SERVES 4–6.

Note: If you prefer, use slices or fillets of fish.

Fried Fish with Sweet-Sour Sauce

3 *pound bass or carp*
1 *teaspoon dry sherry*
1 *teaspoon soy sauce*
2 *teaspoons salt*
½ *teaspoon monosodium glutamate*
⅛ *teaspoon black pepper*
3 *tablespoons finely chopped onion*
3 *teaspoons chopped ginger root or 1 teaspoon ground ginger*

½ *cup cornstarch*
vegetable oil for deep frying
¾ *cup cider vinegar*
¼ *cup sugar*
1 *green or sweet red pepper, cut julienne*
1 *carrot, cut julienne*
3 *green onions, thinly sliced*
2 *tablespoons thinly sliced mixed sweet pickles*

Split and bone the fish, leaving the head and tail on. Sprinkle with the sherry, soy sauce, 1 teaspoon salt, monosodium glutamate, pepper, onion and ½ of the ginger. Rub into the fish and let stand ½ hour. Roll fish in the cornstarch (reserve 1 tablespoon) and let dry for 5 minutes. Fry the fish in hot (350°) oil 15 minutes. Drain. Combine the vinegar, sugar, 1 tablespoon cornstarch, green or red pepper, carrot, green onion and pickles. Mix in remaining salt and ginger. Cook over low heat, stirring steadily, until thickened. Pour this sauce over the fried fish.

⟨[SERVES 4.

Sweet-and-Sour Sliced Fish

4 slices white-meat fish,   ½ cup diced carrot,
   ½-inch thick   optional
5 tablespoons cornstarch   1 cup green peas, optional
2 tablespoons dry sherry   5 tablespoons sugar
½ teaspoon ground ginger   4 tablespoons vinegar
6 tablespoons soy sauce   ½ teaspoon salt
2¼ cups vegetable oil   1 cup water

Cut 2 gashes on each edge of the fish slices. Combine
4 tablespoons cornstarch, the sherry, ginger and 2 tablespoons soy sauce. Dip fish in the mixture. In a deep skillet
heat 2 cups oil until it bubbles. Fry the fish until crisp
and brown on both sides. Drain.

Heat 4 tablespoons oil in a skillet. If you use the carrots
and green peas sauté them in the oil 3 minutes. Stir in
the sugar, vinegar, salt, and remaining soy sauce and bring
to a boil. Mix the remaining cornstarch with the water
and add to the skillet, stirring constantly until the mixture
thickens. Pour the sauce over the fish.

⟮ SERVES 4.

Braised Fish Fillets

3 tablespoons vegetable oil   2 cups bean sprouts
1 pound fish fillets, cut in ¼ cup water
   bite-size pieces   2 tablespoons soy sauce
1 teaspoon salt   8 green onions, cut
½ teaspoon black pepper   in ½-inch pieces
½ teaspoon ground ginger

Heat the oil in a skillet; add the fish, salt, pepper and
ginger. Cook until fish browns lightly. Remove the fish.
To the oil remaining in the skillet, add the bean sprouts,

water and soy sauce. Bring to a boil and cook 2 minutes. Return the fish and add the green onions; mix lightly and cook 3 minutes.

《 SERVES 4–6.

Fried Fish Fillets

1 *pound fish fillets*
4 *tablespoons dry sherry*
1 *teaspoon salt*
⅛ *teaspoon black pepper*
4 *tablespoons cornstarch*
2 *egg whites*
vegetable oil for deep frying

Cut the fillets into pieces 1½ inches long and ½ inch wide. Sprinkle with the sherry, then with the salt and pepper, and finally with 2 tablespoons cornstarch. Beat the egg white, add the remaining cornstarch and beat until stiff but not dry. Dip fish in egg-white mixture. Heat the oil to 370°. Fry a few pieces at a time until very pale yellow. Drain.

《 SERVES 4–6.

Nut-Fish Cakes

¾ *pound fish fillets (sole, flounder or cod)*
¾ *pound raw shrimp, shelled and deveined*
3 *slices bacon*
1 *cup ground peanuts*
2 *tablespoons cornstarch*
1 *tablespoon soy sauce*
1 *teaspoon salt*
1 *egg white*
1 *cup vegetable oil*

Grind the fish, shrimp and bacon through the fine blade of a food chopper, or chop very fine. Mix in the nuts, cornstarch, soy sauce, salt, egg white and 1 tablespoon oil until thoroughly blended. Form heaping tablespoons of the mixture into flat patties. Heat the remaining oil in a skillet until it bubbles. Fry the patties in it until browned on both sides. Serve hot.

《 MAKES ABOUT 24.

Fried Shrimp with Spicy Sauce

1 *pound raw shrimp,*
  shelled and deveined
1 *tablespoon cornstarch*
vegetable oil for deep frying
1 *tablespoon soy sauce*
1 *tablespoon dry sherry*
2 *tablespoons sugar*
1 *teaspoon salt*
¼ *teaspoon Tabasco*
¼ *teaspoon monosodium*
  glutamate
3 *tablespoons vegetable oil*
1 *clove garlic, minced*
2 *slices ginger root or ½*
  teaspoon ground ginger

Cut each shrimp in four and dust with cornstarch. Heat the oil to 370°; fry the shrimp until they turn pink. Drain. Combine the soy sauce, sherry, sugar, salt, Tabasco and monosodium glutamate in a bowl. Heat the 3 tablespoons oil in a skillet and sauté garlic and ginger 2 minutes. Add the soy sauce mixture and bring to a boil. Add the shrimp, stir well and cook for 2 minutes.

《 SERVES 4–6.

Braised Shrimp in Tomato Sauce

1 *pound raw shrimp,*
  shelled and deveined
1 *teaspoon dry sherry*
2 *tablespoons corn-*
  starch
2¼ *cups vegetable oil*
½ *cup chopped onion*
2 *teaspoons chopped*
  ginger root or ¾
  teaspoon ground ginger
1⅓ *teaspoons salt*
2 *teaspoons sugar*
4 *tablespoons ketchup*
¾ *cup water*

Toss shrimp with the sherry and 1 tablespoon cornstarch. Heat 2 cups oil in a skillet; fry the shrimp in it until they turn pink. Drain and pour off oil. Heat remaining oil and sauté the onion and ginger 5 minutes. Return shrimp to pan. Mix together the salt, sugar, ketchup, water and remaining cornstarch and add, stirring constantly until thickened.

(SERVES 4–6.

Breaded Shrimp in Tomato Sauce

1½ pounds raw shrimp, shelled and deveined
½ cup cornstarch
2 eggs, beaten
1 cup dry breadcrumbs
1 quart vegetable oil
¾ cup sliced green onion
¼ cup diced bamboo shoots or water chestnuts

1 clove garlic, minced
1 teaspoon minced preserved ginger or ½ teaspoon ground
1 cup water
¼ cup ketchup
2 tablespoons sugar
2 teaspoons soy sauce
1 teaspoon cider vinegar

Wash and dry the shrimp. Toss in the cornstarch (reserve 1 tablespoon), dip in the eggs, then roll in the breadcrumbs. Heat the oil (reserve 3 tablespoons) to 365°. Fry the shrimp in it until golden brown. Drain, place on a serving dish and keep warm. Heat the reserved 3 tablespoons oil in a skillet; sauté the green onion, bamboo shoots or water chestnuts, garlic and ginger 3 minutes. Mix the reserved cornstarch with the water. Add the ketchup, sugar, soy sauce and vinegar. Add to the skillet and stir until thickened. Pour over the shrimp and serve hot.

(SERVES 4–6.

Sautéed Shrimp with Green Peas

1 *pound raw shrimp,*
shelled and deveined
3 *tablespoons dry*
sherry
1 *egg white*
2 *tablespoons cornstarch*

3 *tablespoons*
vegetable oil
2 *teaspoons sugar*
1½ *teaspoons salt*
1 *8-ounce can green peas,*
drained

Toss the shrimp in a mixture of 1 tablespoon sherry, the unbeaten egg white and the cornstarch. Heat the oil in a skillet and sauté shrimp until pink. Add the sugar, salt, remaining sherry and the green peas and mix well. Cook 2 minutes. Serve hot.

(SERVES 4–6.

Sautéed Shrimp with Green Peppers

1½ *pounds raw shrimp,*
shelled and deveined
3 *green peppers*
2 *tomatoes*
¼ *cup vegetable oil*
1½ *teaspoons salt*
¼ *teaspoon black pepper*

½ *teaspoon ground ginger*
1 *clove garlic, minced*
½ *cup boiling water*
2 *tablespoons soy sauce*
1 *egg, beaten*
¼ *cup thinly sliced green*
onion

Wash and dry the shrimp. Cut each pepper in 8 pieces lengthwise, discarding the seeds and fibers. Cut each tomato in 6 wedges.

Heat the oil in a deep skillet; add the shrimp, salt, pepper, ginger and garlic; cook over low heat 2 minutes, stirring constantly. Add the peppers; cook 1 minute, still stirring. Add the water and soy sauce; cover, bring to a boil and cook 3 minutes. Mix in the tomatoes; cook 3 minutes. Stir in the egg and green onion; cook 1 minute.

(SERVES 6–8.

Shrimp in Black Bean Sauce

1 *tablespoon Chinese black beans*
2 *tablespoons vegetable oil*
1 *clove garlic, minced*
1 *pound raw shrimp, shelled and deveined*
1 *tablespoon cornstarch*
½ *cup water*
3 *green onions, thinly sliced*

Thoroughly wash the beans, drain well and crush. Heat the oil in a skillet and sauté the garlic and shrimp 3 minutes. Combine the beans, cornstarch and water and mix into the shrimp, stirring constantly. Mix in the green onions, cover and cook over low heat 3 minutes.

❲ SERVES 4–6.

Shrimp and Red and Green Peppers

6 *slices bacon, chopped*
1 *pound raw shrimp, shelled, deveined and diced*
2 *cloves garlic, minced*
4 *peppers (red and green) cut in ½-inch squares*
¼ *teaspoon dried ground red peppers*
3 *teaspoons anchovy paste*
2 *tablespoons soy sauce*
½ *teaspoon sugar*
½ *teaspoon monosodium glutamate*
¼ *teaspoon cinnamon*
½ *cup water*

Fry the bacon 2 minutes. Drain off fat. Add the shrimp, garlic, peppers, dried peppers and sauté 2 minutes. Combine the anchovy paste, soy sauce, sugar, monosodium glutamate, cinnamon and water and stir in. Cover and cook over low heat 10 minutes.

❲ SERVES 4–6.

Barbecued Shrimp

1 *pound raw shrimp*
2 *tablespoons dry sherry*
2 *tablespoons soy sauce*
4 *tablespoons chopped green onion*
½ *teaspoon ground ginger*

2 *tablespoons sugar*
1 *tablespoon sesame-seed oil or vegetable oil*
½ *teaspoon salt*
¼ *teaspoon monosodium glutamate*

Wash shrimp, slit back and devein, but do not remove shells. Combine remaining ingredients and marinate shrimp in the mixture for 30 minutes. Drain and bake in a 400° oven for 10 minutes or fry in 6 tablespoons oil 8 minutes. Serve cold.

(SERVES 4.

Shrimp and Green Peas

2 *tablespoons vegetable oil*
2 *pounds raw shrimp, shelled and deveined*
¼ *cup chopped green onion*
1 *teaspoon minced garlic*
2 *teaspoons minced ginger root or 1 teaspoon ground ginger*

1½ *cups canned or cooked frozen green peas, drained*
2 *teaspoons cornstarch*
1 *teaspoon sugar*
1 *teaspoon salt*
1 *teaspoon monosodium glutamate*
1 *teaspoon soy sauce*
¾ *cup chicken broth*

Heat the oil in a skillet and sauté the shrimp, green onion, garlic and ginger root 3 minutes. Add the peas and cook 1 minute. Mix together the cornstarch, sugar, salt, monosodium glutamate, soy sauce and chicken broth. Add to the shrimp and stir until thickened.

(SERVES 6–8.

Fried Shrimp with Pineapple

1 cup sifted flour	vegetable oil for deep frying
1 teaspoon baking powder	1 8-ounce can pineapple
1½ teaspoons salt	chunks
1 egg, beaten	1 tablespoon sugar
½ cup water	1 tablespoon cornstarch
1 pound raw shrimp,	4 tablespoons cider
shelled and deveined	vinegar

Sift the flour, baking powder and ½ teaspoon salt into a bowl. Beat in the egg and water. Dip the shrimp in this batter, coating well, and fry in hot (370°) oil until browned all over. Drain.

Heat the pineapple and drain, reserving the syrup. Combine the sugar, cornstarch, vinegar and remaining salt. Mix in the pineapple syrup. Cook over low heat, stirring constantly, until thickened. Arrange shrimp and pineapple chunks on a serving dish and pour the sauce over them.

❖ SERVES 4–6.

Crabmeat, Cantonese Style

¼ cup vegetable oil	1 teaspoon sugar
½ pound ground pork	½ cup hot chicken broth
1 teaspoon salt	1 pound lump crabmeat
½ teaspoon white pepper	1 egg, beaten
1 clove garlic, minced	¼ cup thinly sliced green
2 tablespoons soy sauce	onion

Heat the oil in a skillet; add the pork, salt, pepper and garlic. Cook over low heat, stirring constantly, until browned. Mix in the soy sauce, sugar and broth; cook 2 minutes. Carefully mix in the crabmeat; cook 3 minutes. Remove from heat and gently mix in the egg and green onion.

❖ SERVES 4–6.

Crab Shreds

1 pound lump crabmeat	¼ cup sliced green onion
3 tablespoons vegetable oil	4 tablespoons dry sherry
2 thin slices ginger root or	4 tablespoons soy sauce
½ teaspoon ground ginger	1 teaspoon sugar

Pick over the crabmeat, removing any shell. Heat the oil in a skillet nad sauté the crabmeat and ginger root 2 minutes (if using ground ginger do not add yet). Stir in the green onion, sherry, soy sauce and sugar. Add ground ginger. Cook over low heat, stirring frequently, until liquid is absorbed.

(SERVES 4–6.

Crabmeat and Pork

1 pound lump crabmeat	2 tablespoons water
3 tablespoons vegetable oil	1 tablespoon dry sherry
¼ pound pork, minced	1 teaspoon salt
2 eggs, beaten	½ teaspoon sugar
2 tablespoons soy sauce	¼ cup chopped green onion

Pick over the crabmeat, removing any shell. Heat the oil in a skillet and sauté the pork 5 minutes. Stir in the eggs, then immediately add the soy sauce, water, sherry, salt, sugar and crabmeat. Mix thoroughly and cook over low heat 3 minutes. Serve sprinkled with the green onion.

(SERVES 4–6.

Braised Crabmeat and Vegetables

1½ cups chicken broth
1 teaspoon salt
1 cup shredded cabbage
1 cup green beans, cut in 3-inch lengths
1 cup green peas
3 tablespoons vegetable oil
1 pound crabmeat, flaked
1 tablespoon dry sherry
1 teaspoon minced ginger root or ½ teaspoon ground ginger
1 teaspoon cornstarch
1 tablespoon soy sauce

Bring the broth to a boil in a saucepan; add the salt and vegetables and cook 5 minutes. Heat the oil in a skillet and sauté the crabmeat ½ minute. Add the sherry and ginger. Mix the cornstarch and soy sauce, add to crabmeat mixture and stir until thickened. Add to the vegetable mixture. Cook 1 minute.

❮ SERVES 4–6.

Peppers Stuffed with Shellfish

4 green peppers
1½ pounds crabmeat or shrimp, chopped
8 hard-cooked eggs, chopped
1 teaspoon salt
½ teaspoon ground ginger
2 tablespoons vegetable oil
½ cup chicken broth
1 tablespoon soy sauce

Wash the peppers, cut in half lengthwise and scoop out the seeds and fibers. Mix together the crabmeat or shrimp, eggs, salt and ginger. Stuff the pepper halves. Arrange in a skillet and add a mixture of the oil, broth and soy sauce. Bring to a boil, cover and cook over low heat 20 minutes. Serve hot.

❮ SERVES 4–8.

Steamed Lobster

2 1¼-pound live lobsters	½ teaspoon black pepper
or 4 African lobster tails	2 tablespoons soy sauce
¼ pound ground pork	½ teaspoon sugar
3 eggs, beaten	2 tablespoons vegetable oil
1 teaspoon salt	

Have the live lobsters cut up in the shell into 1-inch pieces, the claws in 3 pieces. Or cut the lobster tails crosswise into 1-inch pieces. Place in a shallow baking dish in a single layer. Mix together all the remaining ingredients and spread over the lobsters.

Place the baking dish on a rack in a deep pan and add boiling water to just reach the rack. Cover the pan, bring to a boil and cook over low heat 40 minutes.

❴ SERVES 2–4.

Cantonese Lobster

2 live lobsters, 1½ pounds each	2 teaspoons minced ginger root or 1 teaspoon ground ginger
3 tablespoons vegetable oil	
¼ pound raw pork, ground	3 green onions, chopped
2 tablespoons corn- starch	1 clove garlic, minced
	1 teaspoon salt
2 tablespoons dry sherry	2 eggs, beaten
2 tablespoons soy sauce	½ cup water

Have the lobsters split, cleaned, and cut, in shell, into 1½-inch pieces, and claws into 3 pieces. Heat the oil in a deep skillet and sauté the pork 5 minutes, stirring frequently. Add the lobster and cook 10 minutes, stirring frequently. Combine the cornstarch, sherry, soy sauce, ginger root or ground ginger, green onions, garlic, salt.

eggs and water. Mix into lobsters, stirring constantly for 3 minutes.

(⟮ SERVES 2–4.

Fried Oysters

20 *shucked oysters*   1 *teaspoon baking powder*
 1 *teaspoon salt*   1 *tablespoon vegetable oil*
 1 *tablespoon dry sherry*   1 *cup water (about)*
 1 *cup sifted flour*   *vegetable oil for deep frying*
 4 *tablespoons cornstarch*

Wash and drain the oysters. Pour boiling water over them, drain and cool. Sprinkle with the salt and sherry. Sift the flour, cornstarch and baking powder into a bowl and mix in the 1 tablespoon oil and the water (you may not need all the water) to form a thick batter. Dip the oysters in the batter and fry in hot (370°) oil until golden brown. Drain and serve hot.

(⟮ SERVES 4–6.

Meat

6

Meat

Chinese Fresh Ham

4- to 5-pound fresh ham
1 cup water
4 green onions, cut in
  2-inch lengths
1 teaspoon ground ginger
2 cups soy sauce

¼ teaspoon anise
½ cup dry sherry
1 tablespoon sugar
1 clove garlic, crushed
6 hard-cooked eggs, halved

Rinse the ham in cold water and dry with paper towels. Bring 1 cup water to a boil and add the green onions, ginger, soy sauce, anise, sherry, sugar and garlic. Add the ham and enough water to cover. Bring to a boil, cover, and then simmer 3 hours or until tender. Remove meat, slice and arrange on a heated platter. Garnish with the hard-cooked egg halves. Skim the fat from the cooking liquid. Put 2 cups of the liquid into a saucepan, bring to a boil and thicken with a paste made of 1 tablespoon cornstarch and a little cold water. Simmer 2 minutes and serve separately as a sauce. Rice or noodles are appropriate accompaniments.

⟦ SERVES 10–12.

Spareribs with Pineapple Sauce

2 racks spareribs (about 4 pounds)

½ cup soy sauce

1 16-ounce can pineapple chunks

¾ cup sugar

1 cup cider vinegar

4 small white onions, quartered

1 green pepper, cut julienne

1 carrot, cut julienne

1 tablespoon cornstarch

2 tablespoons dry sherry

2 tablespoons chopped preserved ginger or 2 teaspoons ground ginger

Trim the spareribs of all the fat and brush with the soy sauce, reserving 2 tablespoons. Place on a rack in a shallow roasting pan and roast in a 375° oven 1¼ hours, turning them frequently to brown all sides. Drain the pineapple, reserving ½ cup juice. Mix together the reserved juice, sugar, vinegar, onions, green pepper and carrot. Bring to a boil and cook over low heat 3 minutes. Mix together the cornstarch, sherry and remaining soy sauce. Stir into the sauce, stirring constantly until thickened and clear. Add ¾ cup pineapple and the ginger. Heat.

Cut the pork into individual ribs and pour sauce over them.

⟨[SERVES 6–8.

Sweet-and-Sour Pork Chops

6 pork chops, cut 1 inch thick

1½ teaspoons salt

½ teaspoon black pepper

½ teaspoon ground ginger

¼ cup flour

2 tablespoons vegetable oil

½ cup chopped onion

1 clove garlic, minced

⅓ cup chili sauce

2 teaspoons soy sauce

3 tablespoons cider vinegar

1½ tablespoons brown sugar

¾ cup boiling water

Trim the fat from the chops and pound lightly to flatten. Dip in a mixture of the salt, pepper, ginger and flour. Heat the oil in a deep skillet with an ovenproof handle. Brown the chops in it. Add the onion and garlic; cook 5 minutes. Pour off the fat. Mix together the chili sauce, soy sauce, vinegar, sugar and water; add to the skillet. Cover and bake in a 375° oven 50 minutes, removing the cover for the last 10 minutes.

◖ SERVES 6.

Sweet-and-Sour Pork

2 *pounds boneless pork*
⅓ *cup cornstarch*
4 *tablespoons dry sherry*
½ *cup soy sauce*
2 *cups vegetable oil*
2 *large onions, each cut in six wedges*
4 *green peppers, cut in strips*
1 *carrot, thinly sliced*
½ *cup diced water chestnuts*
¾ *cup canned pineapple chunks*
½ *cup sugar*
⅓ *cup ketchup*
3 *tablespoons cider vinegar*
¾ *cup water*

Cut the pork in 1-inch cubes. Toss in a mixture of 4 tablespoons of the cornstarch, 2 tablespoons of the sherry and 4 tablespoons of the soy sauce. Heat the oil in a skillet; fry the pork until browned on all sides and tender. Drain the pork and keep hot; pour off all but ¼ cup oil. In the oil remaining in the skillet, sauté the onions, green peppers and carrots 3 minutes. Add the water chestnuts and pineapple; cook 2 minutes.

Mix together the sugar, ketchup, vinegar and the remaining sherry and soy sauce. Add to the skillet and bring to a boil. Stir in the water mixed with the remaining cornstarch. Cook, stirring constantly, until thickened. Add the pork, mix well, heat and serve.

◖ SERVES 6–8.

Batter-Fried Sweet-and-Pungent Pork

1 *pound boneless pork*
  shoulder
1 *egg*
½ *teaspoon salt*
½ *cup flour*
1¼ *cups water*
vegetable oil for deep frying

½ *cup cider vinegar*
¼ *cup brown sugar*
1 *tablespoon molasses*
2 *tablespoons cornstarch*
1 *8-ounce can pineapple*
  wedges, drained
1 *tomato, cut in 6 wedges*

Cut the pork in 1-inch cubes. Beat the egg and salt; mix in the flour and ¼ cup of the water until a smooth batter is formed. Dip the pork cubes in the mixture, coating the pieces on all sides. Heat the oil to 365°. Fry the pork until browned on all sides. Don't crowd the pan. Drain and keep hot. In a saucepan, mix the vinegar, brown sugar, molasses and ¾ cup of the water. Bring to a boil. Mix the cornstarch with the remaining water; stir into the sauce until thickened. Add the pineapple and tomato; cook over low heat 3 minutes. Mix in the pork and serve.

❲ SERVES 4.

Pork Balls and Cabbage

1 *pound ground pork*
¼ *cup chopped green onion*
½ *cup chopped water*
  chestnuts
1 *teaspoon salt*
½ *teaspoon ground ginger*
1 *egg, beaten*

3 *tablespoons soy sauce*
4 *tablespoons dry sherry*
¼ *cup cornstarch*
½ *cup vegetable oil*
2 *pounds Chinese or green*
  cabbage, shredded
1½ *cups water*

With a fork, mix together the pork, green onion, water chestnuts, salt, ginger, egg, 1 tablespoon soy sauce and 1 tablespoon sherry. Shape into 6 balls and roll lightly in the cornstarch. Heat the oil in a deep skillet; brown the pork balls in it. Remove. In the oil remaining in the skillet, fry the cabbage for 5 minutes, stirring frequently. Arrange the pork balls over the cabbage and add the water mixed with the remaining sherry and soy sauce. Cover and cook over low heat 1 hour.

([SERVES 6.

Sweet-and-Sour Pork Balls

1 *pound ground pork*	4 *tablespoons cornstarch*
4 *green onions, chopped*	3 *cups vegetable oil*
½ *teaspoon ground ginger*	¾ *cup sliced, cooked carrots*
2 *tablespoons dry sherry*	1 *package frozen snow peas*
5 *tablespoons soy sauce*	5 *tablespoons sugar*
1 *teaspoon salt*	4 *tablespoons cider vinegar*
½ *teaspoon monosodium*	½ *cup beef broth*
glutamate	1 *cup water*
1 *egg*	

Mix together the pork, green onions, ginger, 1 tablespoon sherry, 2 tablespoons soy sauce, ½ teaspoon salt, monosodium glutamate, egg and 2 tablespoons cornstarch. Shape tablespoons of the mixture into balls. Heat 2¾ cups oil in a skillet until it bubbles. Fry the balls until browned. Drain.

Heat the remaining oil in a skillet and sauté the carrots and snow peas 3 minutes. Combine the sugar, vinegar, beef broth and the remaining soy sauce, salt and sherry. Pour over the vegetables and bring to a boil. Add the pork balls, then add remaining cornstarch mixed with the water and stir until thickened.

([SERVES 4–6.

Pork Chow Mein

2 tablespoons	3 tablespoons soy sauce
vegetable oil	1 19-ounce can bean sprouts,
1½ cups sliced onion	drained
1½ cups sliced celery	3 tablespoons cornstarch
2 cups diced cooked pork	2 cups beef broth

Heat the oil in a deep skillet; sauté the onion and celery
5 minutes. Mix in the pork, soy sauce and sprouts; cook
2 minutes. Mix the cornstarch with the broth; add to the
skillet, stirring steadily to the boiling point; cook 3 minutes
longer. Serve with rice and chow mein noodles.

(SERVES 4–6.

Chop Suey

Chop Suey is really a Chinese-American dish, but it is
served in so many restaurants in the United States that
it is included in this book.

1 pound boneless pork, or	2 tablespoons soy sauce
beef, or raw, cleaned	1 tablespoon molasses
shrimp	2 cups hot beef broth
3 tablespoons vegetable oil	1 10-ounce can bean
1 teaspoon salt	sprouts
½ teaspoon black pepper	3 tablespoons cornstarch
2 large onions	¼ cup water
1 bunch celery	

Cut the pork or beef in ¼-inch cubes, or dice the shrimp,
if you are using them. Heat the oil, salt and pepper in a
skillet. Add the pork, beef or shrimp. Cook over medium
heat 5 minutes, stirring frequently. (If shrimp are used,
remove from pan at this point.) Cut each onion in 6
wedges and the celery in 1-inch pieces. Mix into the

skillet with the soy sauce. Cook over low heat, stirring almost constantly. Mix in the molasses and broth. Cover and cook over low heat 15 minutes. Add the sprouts; cook 3 minutes. Mix the cornstarch with the water and add to the skillet, stirring constantly until thickened. (Return shrimp to skillet at this point.) Cook 2 minutes more. Serve with rice.

（[SERVES 4–6.

Taiwan Pork

1 *pound boneless pork*

3 *tablespoons vegetable oil*

1½ *cups chopped onion*

2 *cups shredded celery cabbage*

3 *tablespoons soy sauce*

1½ *cups julienne-cut green peppers*

1 *teaspoon sugar*

½ *teaspoon ground ginger*

Cut the pork in ¼-inch cubes. Heat the oil in a skillet; add the pork and onions. Cook over medium heat, stirring frequently, until browned. Mix in the cabbage and soy sauce; cook 10 minutes, stirring frequently. Add the green peppers, sugar and ginger; cook 5 minutes.

（[SERVES 4–6.

Braised Pork and Spinach

6-rib *pork loin, boned (about 3 pounds)*

1 *clove garlic, minced*

1 *teaspoon salt*

¼ *teaspoon black pepper*

2 *tablespoons honey*

¼ *cup soy sauce*

1 *cup boiling beef broth*

2 *tablespoons dry sherry*

2 *packages frozen leaf spinach, thawed*

Rub the pork with the garlic, salt and pepper. In a deep skillet or heavy saucepan, brown the pork on all sides.

Pour off all but 2 tablespoons fat. Mix the honey, soy sauce, broth and sherry; pour over the pork. Cover and cook over low heat 1½ hours, or until tender. Baste and turn meat frequently. Remove the meat. Cook the spinach in the gravy 2 minutes. Heap the spinach in the center of a serving dish, slice the pork thin and arrange over the spinach.

(SERVES 4–6.

Pork and Green Beans

1 pound green beans or 1 package frozen cut beans
2 tablespoons vegetable oil
1 pound ground pork
1 clove garlic, minced
¾ teaspoon salt
2 tablespoons soy sauce
½ cup sliced water chestnuts
1¼ cups water
2 teaspoons cornstarch
1 cup shredded lettuce
4 green onions, sliced

Wash the beans and cut crosswise into ¼-inch slices. Or cut the thawed frozen beans the same way. Heat the oil in a skillet; add the pork and garlic. Cook over medium heat, stirring constantly, until browned. Add the salt, soy sauce and water chestnuts. Cook 1 minute. Add 1 cup water; bring to a boil and gradually stir in the green beans. Cook 1 minute, cover and cook 2 minutes. Mix the cornstarch with the remaining water, add to the skillet and stir until thickened. Put the lettuce in a deep, hot serving dish and pour the meat mixture over it. Sprinkle with the green onions.

(SERVES 4–6.

Fried Pork with Green Onions

1½ *pounds boneless pork*
¼ *cup soy sauce*
2 *tablespoons dry*
sherry

5 *tablespoons vegetable oil*
3 *bunches green onions,*
cut in 2-inch pieces
1 *teaspoon salt*

Cut the pork in paper-thin 1-inch pieces. Toss with the soy sauce and sherry. Heat the oil in a skillet and sauté the pork until no pink remains. Add the green onions and salt. Cook over high heat 30 seconds, stirring constantly.

《 SERVES 4–6.

Braised Pork with Broccoli

3 *tablespoons vegetable oil*
2 *pounds pork, cut in*
1-inch cubes
1 *clove garlic, minced*
2 *teaspoons minced ginger*
root or ½ teaspoon
ground ginger

¾ *cup soy sauce*
2 *tablespoons sherry*
1 *teaspoon sugar*
½ *cup water*
1 *pound fresh broccoli or*
2 packages frozen, thawed
and chopped

Heat 2 tablespoons oil in a deep skillet and brown the pork all over. Stir in the garlic, ginger, soy sauce, sherry, sugar and water. Bring to a boil. Cover and cook over low heat 1½ hours. Heat remaining oil in a saucepan and cook the broccoli over high heat 4 minutes. Drain. Arrange on a serving dish and top with the pork.

《 SERVES 6–8.

Pork with Bamboo Shoots

1 *pound boneless pork*	¼ *cup vegetable oil*
2 *tablespoons cornstarch*	¼ *cup sliced green onion*
1 *tablespoon dry sherry*	1 *cup diced bamboo shoots*
6 *tablespoons soy sauce*	2 *teaspoons sugar*

Chop the pork coarsely, dip in the cornstarch, then into a mixture of the sherry and half the soy sauce.

Heat the oil in a skillet; add the pork and green onion. Sauté until pork browns. Add the bamboo shoots, sugar and remaining soy sauce. Cook over low heat 10 minutes, stirring frequently.

(SERVES 4–6.

Fragrant Pork

2 *pounds boneless pork*	1 *cup dry sherry*
1 *cup soy sauce*	¾ *cup beef broth*

Cut the pork into 1½-inch cubes. Use a saucepan with a tight-fitting cover. Combine all the ingredients in it. Cover. Place saucepan in a larger pan and add boiling water to reach halfway up the smaller pan. Cover the large pan and cook 4 hours, adding boiling water if necessary to keep level up.

(SERVES 4–6.

Fried Pork Chops

6 *pork chops, cut ¼-inch thick and boned*	½ *teaspoon ground ginger*
	2 *tablespoons vegetable oil*
½ *cup soy sauce*	¼ *cup sliced green onion*
1 *tablespoon dry sherry*	1 *tablespoon sugar*
1 *clove garlic, minced*	⅛ *teaspoon black pepper*

Marinate the chops in a mixture of 3 tablespoons soy sauce, the sherry, garlic and ginger for 30 minutes. Drain. Heat the oil in a skillet and sauté the chops until golden brown on both sides. Add the green onion, sugar, pepper and remaining soy sauce. Cover and cook over low heat 20 minutes or until the chops are tender.

([SERVES 3–6.

Pork and Noodles

1½ *pounds boneless pork*
4 *tablespoons vegetable oil*
2 *teaspoons salt*
¼ *teaspoon black pepper*
2 *cups bean sprouts*
2 *cups sliced celery*
2 *cups sliced Chinese cabbage*

4 *tablespoons soy sauce*
1 *teaspoon sugar*
2 *tablespoons cornstarch*
1½ *cups chicken broth*
3 *cups cooked and drained fine noodles*
¼ *cup chopped green onion*

Cut the pork into julienne strips. Heat the oil in a deep skillet and sauté the pork 5 minutes. Mix in the salt, pepper, bean sprouts, celery, Chinese cabbage, soy sauce and sugar. Cover and cook over low heat 5 minutes. Blend the cornstarch and chicken broth, add to the skillet and stir until thickened. Lightly mix in the noodles and heat through. Sprinkle with the green onion.

([SERVES 4–6.
Note: Chicken may be substituted for the pork.

Barbecued Fillet Mignon

1 *pound fillet of beef*
4 *tablespoons soy sauce*
2 *tablespoons dry sherry*
1 *teaspoon ground ginger*
1 *teaspoon sugar*
⅛ *teaspoon black pepper*

½ *cup vegetable oil*
2 *pounds spinach, shredded, or 2 packages frozen, thawed*
1 *teaspoon salt*

Cut the meat in ¼-inch-thick slices. Mix the soy sauce, sherry, ginger, sugar and pepper. Marinate the beef in it for 2 hours. Drain. Heat 3 tablespoons oil in a skillet and fry the spinach 3 minutes, stirring frequently. Season with the salt.

In a separate skillet, heat the remaining oil. Sauté the beef over high heat 4 minutes, turning the slices once. Arrange spinach on a hot serving dish, arrange beef on top and pour juices from sautéed beef over all.

❲ SERVES 4.

Sautéed Sliced Beef

1 *pound beef, cut in*   ⅓ *cup soy sauce*
    bite-size pieces   2 *tablespoons*
2 *green onions, chopped*   *sugar*
1 *clove garlic, minced*   2 *tablespoons sesame-*
¼ *teaspoon dried ground*   *seed or vegetable oil*
    red chili peppers

Combine the beef, green onions, garlic, red pepper, soy sauce, sugar and oil. Soak 15 minutes. Remove beef from marinade and sauté in an ungreased skillet over high heat until lightly browned.

❲ SERVES 4–6.

Beef and Onions

1½ *pounds sirloin steak*   ½ *teaspoon sugar*
5 *tablespoons*   2 *tablespoons soy sauce*
    vegetable oil   2 *tablespoons dry sherry*
4 *cups sliced onion*   2 *tablespoons cornstarch*

Have the steak pounded ¼-inch thick, then cut into narrow strips. Heat half the oil in a skillet and sauté the onion 3 minutes. Add the sugar, 1 tablespoon soy sauce and 1 tablespoon sherry. Bring to boil. Remove onion from pan. Toss the steak with the cornstarch, remaining soy sauce and the sherry. Add the remaining oil to the pan and brown the steak quickly over high heat. Return onion mixture to pan and cook 2 minutes.

⟨ SERVES 4–6.

Sautéed Beef with Snow Peas

1 *pound snow peas*	2 *tablespoons cornstarch*
1½ *pounds sirloin steak,*	¾ *cup vegetable oil*
cut in bite-size pieces	2 *cloves garlic, minced*
3 *tablespoons dry sherry*	1 *teaspoon sugar*
½ *cup soy sauce*	

Remove the end tips from the snow peas and cook in boiling water 3 minutes, or until tender but still crisp. Toss the beef with the sherry, 3 tablespoons soy sauce and the cornstarch. Heat ½ cup oil in a skillet and sauté beef until lightly browned. Remove. Heat the remaining oil in another skillet and sauté the snow peas 2 minutes. Stir in the beef, garlic, sugar and remaining soy sauce. Mix well.

⟨ SERVES 4–6.

Sautéed Beef and Green Peppers

1 *pound sirloin steak*	½ *cup vegetable oil*
¼ *teaspoon black pepper*	3 *cups julienne-cut green*
1 *tablespoon cornstarch*	*peppers*
4 *tablespoons soy sauce*	1 *teaspoon salt*

Cut the steak in paper-thin pieces 1 inch square. Toss with the pepper, cornstarch and 2 tablespoons soy sauce. Heat half the oil in a skillet; add the peppers and salt; sauté until browned. Transfer to a plate. Heat the remaining oil in the skillet. Brown the meat in it. Return the peppers and add the remaining soy sauce. Cook 2 minutes, stirring almost constantly.

SERVES 4–6.

Beef with Cauliflower and Peas

- *1 pound sirloin steak, sliced ¼-inch thick*
- *3 tablespoons vegetable oil*
- *1 clove garlic*
- *½ cup diced onion*
- *1½ teaspoons salt*
- *¼ teaspoon black pepper*
- *1 cup beef broth*
- *1 package frozen cauliflower, thawed*
- *1 package frozen green peas, thawed*
- *2 tablespoons cornstarch*
- *2 tablespoons soy sauce*

Cut the beef in strips ¼-inch wide by 1 inch long. Heat the oil in a skillet; brown the garlic in it and discard. Add the meat and brown it, stirring frequently. Mix in the onion, salt and pepper for 30 seconds. Add ¾ cup of the broth, the cauliflower and peas. Bring to a boil and cook 3 minutes. Mix the cornstarch and soy sauce with the remaining broth. Add to the skillet, stirring steadily until sauce is thickened.

SERVES 4–6.

Cubed Beef

- *1½ pounds eye round of beef*
- *3 tablespoons vegetable oil*
- *1 clove garlic, minced*
- *¼ cup soy sauce*
- *½ teaspoon salt*
- *⅓ cup oyster sauce*
- *2 teaspoons sugar*
- *1 tablespoon dry sherry*
- *1 cup boiling water*
- *½ cup sliced mushrooms, fresh or canned*
- *¼ cup thinly sliced green onion*

Cut the beef in 1-inch cubes. Heat the oil in a skillet; brown the beef and garlic in it, stirring frequently. Add a mixture of the soy sauce, salt, oyster sauce, sugar and sherry. Mix well and cook over low heat 5 minutes. Add the water; cover and cook over low heat 30 minutes, stirring a few times. Mix in the mushrooms; cook 5 minutes. Add the green onion; cook 1 minute.

❰ SERVES 4–6.

Shredded Beef with Chili Peppers

1 *pound sirloin steak, sliced paper-thin*
3 *tablespoons dry sherry*
3 *tablespoons soy sauce*
1 *teaspoon minced garlic*
1 *teaspoon minced ginger root or ½ teaspoon ground ginger*
1 *cup vegetable oil*
1 *cup grated carrot*
½ *teaspoon dried ground red chili peppers*

Cut the beef in strips ½ inch wide. Mix with the sherry, soy sauce, garlic and ginger and let stand 30 minutes. Heat the oil; add the undrained beef, carrots and chili peppers and fry 2 minutes. Drain off all the oil and continue to cook beef and vegetables 3 minutes longer.

❰ SERVES 4.

Sautéed Shredded Beef with Onions

1 *pound sirloin steak, sliced paper-thin*
1 *tablespoon cornstarch*
4 *tablespoons soy sauce*
¾ *cup vegetable oil*
2 *cups chopped onion*
2 *teaspoons salt*
¼ *teaspoon black pepper*

Cut the beef in strips ½ inch wide. Toss with the cornstarch and 2 tablespoons soy sauce. Heat 4 tablespoons oil in a skillet, add the onion and salt and sauté 3 minutes.

Remove. Heat remaining oil in the skillet. Sauté the meat until lightly browned. Mix in onion, the remaining soy sauce and the pepper, stirring well for 1 minute.

❴ SERVES 4–6.

Sweet-and-Sour Beef

2 eggs
1 clove garlic, minced
1½ pounds sirloin steak,
　½-inch thick, cut
　in ½-inch cubes
½ cup cornstarch
vegetable oil for deep frying
1 20-ounce can pineapple
　chunks

½ cup sugar
¾ cup cider vinegar
1 teaspoon salt
2 cups beef broth
2 tomatoes, each cut
　in 6 wedges
2 green peppers, cut
　julienne

Beat the eggs with the garlic and dip the meat in the mixture. Roll meat in ¼ cup cornstarch and fry in hot (375°) oil for 4 minutes, or until browned. Drain. Drain pineapple, reserving the syrup. Mix remaining cornstarch with the pineapple syrup, then stir in the sugar, vinegar, salt and broth. Stir over low heat until thickened. Mix in the pineapple chunks, beef, tomatoes and green peppers. Cook 4 minutes.

❴ SERVES 6–8.

Sweet-and-Sour Beef Balls

1 pound ground beef	3 tablespoons vegetable oil
1 egg	2 tablespoons soy sauce
1 teaspoon salt	3 tablespoons cider
¼ teaspoon black pepper	vinegar
3 tablespoons chopped	⅓ cup sugar
green onion	⅓ cup water
3 tablespoons cornstarch	2 green peppers, cut
1 8-ounce can pineapple	julienne
wedges	

Mix together the beef, egg, salt, pepper, green onion and 1 tablespoon cornstarch. Shape into marble-sized balls. Drain the pineapple, but reserve the syrup. Heat 2 tablespoons oil in a skillet; brown the meatballs in it. Remove. Add the remaining oil to the skillet. Mix together the remaining cornstarch, the soy sauce, vinegar, sugar, water and pineapple syrup. Add to the skillet, stirring steadily until thickened. Add the pineapple, green peppers and meatballs. Bring to a boil and cook 3 minutes.

◖ SERVES 4–6.

Ground Beef with Fried Vermicelli

1 pound ground beef	4 ounces Chinese
2 tablespoons dry sherry	vermicelli or fine egg
⅓ cup soy sauce	noodles, cooked and
2 cups chopped red or	drained
green peppers	vegetable oil for deep frying
2 tablespoons chopped	½ cup vegetable oil
onion	1 cup beef broth
1 teaspoon salt	½ teaspoon monosodium
2 tablespoons cornstarch	glutamate

Mix together the beef, sherry, soy sauce, red peppers, onion, salt and cornstarch. Cut the lengths of vermicelli into fourths (or, if noodles are used, leave whole) and fry in deep hot (370°) oil 3 minutes. Drain and place in a deep dish.

Heat the ½ cup oil in a skillet and sauté the meat mixture until browned. Add the broth and monosodium glutamate, mix thoroughly and pour over fried vermicelli just before serving.

(［ SERVES 4–6.

Fried Liver with Vegetables

1 *pound calf's or beef liver, sliced*

2 *tablespoons dry sherry*

1 *teaspoon salt*

½ *teaspoon ground ginger*

3 *tablespoons soy sauce*

⅓ *cup flour*

1 *cup vegetable oil*

1 *cup sliced onion*

½ *cup sliced celery*

½ *cup julienne-cut green pepper*

½ *teaspoon sugar*

Cut the liver in bite-size pieces. Marinate in a mixture of the sherry, salt, ginger and 1 tablespoon soy sauce for 15 minutes. Drain and coat with the flour. Heat the oil in a skillet until it bubbles. Fry the liver until browned. Remove the liver. Pour off all but 3 tablespoons oil. Sauté the onion, celery and green pepper 5 minutes. Add the sugar, remaining soy sauce and the liver. Cook 1 minute, stirring constantly.

(［ SERVES 4–6.

Poultry

7

Poultry

Empress Chicken

6 chicken legs and
  6 chicken wings
6 tablespoons vegetable oil
1 green onion, cut in ½-inch
  pieces
4 slices ginger root or 1
  teaspoon ground ginger
1 small bamboo shoot,
  cut into thin slices

½ cup soy sauce
2 tablespoons dry sherry
2 cups chicken broth
1 tablespoon sugar
3 tablespoons green peas,
  fresh or canned
⅛ teaspoon monosodium
  glutamate

Wash and dry chicken. Heat oil in a skillet and sauté green onion and ginger 2 minutes. Add chicken and bamboo shoot and sauté until chicken is lightly browned. Stir in soy sauce and sherry and sufficient broth (about 2 cups) to cover the chicken pieces. Cook 20 minutes. Mix in sugar and cook over low heat 30 minutes, adding green peas 5 minutes before end of cooking time. Mix in monosodium glutamate and serve.

❲ SERVES 6.

Velvet Chicken and Creamed Corn

1 *whole raw chicken breast, minced*	1 *12-ounce can cream-style corn*
1 *tablespoon dry sherry*	1 *tablespoon cornstarch*
1½ *teaspoons salt*	3 *tablespoons water*
2 *egg whites, lightly beaten*	½ *teaspoon monosodium glutamate*
4 *cups chicken broth*	2 *tablespoons chopped ham*

Mix the chicken, sherry, 1 teaspoon salt and beaten egg whites. Bring chicken broth and remaining salt to a boil in a saucepan; add the chicken mixture and corn. Bring to a boil again. Mix the cornstarch and water and add to the hot liquid, stirring constantly for 3 minutes. Add monosodium glutamate. Serve in soup bowls garnished with a sprinkling of chopped ham.

(SERVES 4–6.

Chicken Pot-Roast

3 *pound frying chicken*	2 *tablespoons vegetable oil*
1 *clove garlic, minced*	¾ *cup sliced green onion*
1 *teaspoon minced ginger root or ½ teaspoon ground ginger*	1 *teaspoon salt*
	¼ *teaspoon black pepper*
	¼ *teaspoon sugar*
2 *tablespoons soy sauce*	¾ *cup water*
1 *tablespoon sherry*	2 *teaspoons cornstarch*
6 *dried Chinese mushrooms*	

Dice the chicken liver and gizzard and reserve. Wash the chicken, dry well and rub with a mixture of the garlic, ginger, soy sauce and sherry. Let stand 30 minutes. Soak the mushrooms in warm water 20 minutes. Drain and slice. Heat the oil in a heavy saucepan or Dutch oven and brown the chicken all over. Add the chicken liver and gizzard, mushrooms and green onion. Cook 5 minutes. Stir in the salt, pepper, sugar and water. Cover and cook over low heat 45 minutes, or until chicken is tender. Remove chicken. Blend the cornstarch with a little water and stir into the pan until sauce is thickened. Cut the chicken into small pieces and pour the sauce over it.

❰ SERVES 6–8.

Sweet-and-Sour Chicken

3 whole raw chicken breasts, skinned, boned and cut in 2-inch pieces

4 tablespoons soy sauce

½ cup flour

1 teaspoon salt

2 eggs

3 tablespoons sugar

2 tablespoons cornstarch

¼ cup cider vinegar

2 cups water

2 tablespoons ketchup

¾ cup sliced mixed sweet pickles

vegetable oil for deep frying

Sprinkle the chicken pieces with 2 tablespoons soy sauce. Leave 10 minutes. Beat the flour, salt and eggs until smooth. Dip chicken pieces in this batter and fry in hot (370°) oil until browned. Drain. Combine the sugar, cornstarch, vinegar, water and remaining soy sauce and cook over low heat, stirring until thickened. Mix in the ketchup and pickles and cook 1 minute. Pour over the chicken.

❰ SERVES 4–6.

Chicken and Tomatoes

2 *whole raw chicken breasts, skinned, boned and cut in 1-inch squares*	1 *cup diced onion*
	1 *teaspoon sugar*
	1 *teaspoon salt*
1 *tablespoon sherry*	½ *cup chicken broth*
2 *tablespoons cornstarch*	2 *tomatoes, peeled and cubed*
3 *tablespoons soy sauce*	
½ *cup vegetable oil*	

Toss the chicken with the sherry, 1 tablespoon cornstarch and 2 tablespoons soy sauce. Leave 15 minutes. Heat the oil in a skillet and sauté the chicken 10 minutes. Mix in the onion and sauté 2 minutes. Combine the sugar, salt, remaining soy sauce and cornstarch and the chicken broth. Mix into the skillet and stir until sauce is thickened. Add the tomatoes and heat through.

(SERVES 3–4.

Chicken and Peppers

2 *whole raw chicken breasts, cut in 1-inch squares*	2 *teaspoons cornstarch*
	3 *green-and-red peppers, cut in 1-inch squares*
1 *clove garlic, minced*	½ *cup sliced green onion*
2 *tablespoons soy sauce*	3 *stalks celery, sliced in ½-inch pieces*
3 *tablespoons vegetable oil*	
½ *teaspoon salt*	¼ *teaspoon sugar*
¼ *teaspoon black pepper*	¼ *cup cold water*

Combine the chicken, garlic, 1 tablespoon soy sauce, 1 tablespoon oil, salt and pepper, and 1 teaspoon cornstarch. Let stand 20 minutes. Heat the remaining oil in a skillet and sauté the peppers 3 minutes. Add the green onion and celery and sauté 2 minutes. Transfer to a dish. Add the chicken to the skillet and cook 5 minutes. Mix the remaining soy sauce and cornstarch with the sugar and water. Add to the skillet with the cooked vegetables. Stir over low heat 2 minutes, or until thickened.

⟪ SERVES 2–4.

Chicken with Red and Green Peppers

2 whole chicken breasts, cut into 2-inch squares
3 tablespoons dry sherry
5 tablespoons soy sauce
5 tablespoons cornstarch
vegetable oil for deep frying
5 tablespoons sesame-seed oil
1 clove garlic, crushed
3 slices ginger root or 1 teaspoon ground ginger
3 sweet red peppers, seeded and halved
5 green peppers, seeded and quartered
1 teaspoon sugar
⅛ teaspoon monosodium glutamate
1 tablespoon water

Sprinkle chicken with 1 tablespoon sherry, then with 1 tablespoon soy sauce and finally with 4 tablespoons cornstarch. Fry a few pieces at a time in hot (365°) oil until golden brown. Drain. Heat the 5 tablespoons sesame-seed oil and sauté garlic, ginger and red peppers. Add green peppers and sauté 2 minutes—they should not be too soft. Mix in chicken and cook 3 minutes. Stir in sugar, monosodium glutamate, and remaining sherry and soy sauce. Mix remaining cornstarch with water and stir in until sauce is thickened.

⟪ SERVES 4.

Stewed Chestnut Chicken

6 tablespoons
vegetable oil
2 slices ginger root or ½
teaspoon ground ginger
2 green onions, white part
only, cut in small pieces
3½ pound frying chicken
6 tablespoons soy sauce

1 teaspoon salt
2 tablespoons dry sherry
2 cups water
1 tablespoon sugar
1 pound chestnuts, boiled,
shelled, skinned and
halved

Heat the oil in a skillet and sauté the ginger and green
onion 2 minutes. With a sharp cleaver cut the chicken
into 1½-inch pieces, bone and all, or have the butcher
do it. Add the chicken to the skillet and sauté until lightly
browned. Stir in soy sauce, salt, sherry and water. Cover
and simmer 20 minutes. Mix in sugar and chestnuts and
simmer 15 minutes longer.

(SERVES 4.

Pineapple Chicken

2 whole raw chicken
breasts
2 tablespoons cornstarch
2 tablespoons soy sauce
1½ teaspoons salt
1 tablespoon water
1 8-ounce can pineapple
chunks

6 tablespoons
vegetable oil
1½ cups sliced (lengthwise)
onion
1 cup sliced celery
¾ cup sliced water
chestnuts

Remove the skin and bones and cut the chicken in 1-inch
pieces. Toss in a mixture of the cornstarch, soy sauce, salt
and water. Drain the pineapple, reserving ⅓ cup syrup.
    Heat 2 tablespoons oil in a skillet; sauté the onion

3 minutes, stirring frequently. Remove the onion. Add
1 tablespoon oil to the skillet; sauté the celery and water
chestnuts 3 minutes, stirring frequently. Add to the onion.
Heat the remaining oil in the skillet; sauté the chicken in
it until browned and cooked through, stirring frequently.

Add the pineapple and ⅓ cup syrup and return the
vegetables. Cook, stirring frequently, until mixture boils,
then cook 1 minute longer.

◖ SERVES 4–6.

Steamed Chicken with Pineapple

3½-pound frying chicken,	1 tablespoon sugar
vegetable oil for deep frying	2 tablespoons dry sherry
5 slices ginger root or 1	1 teaspoon salt
teaspoon ground ginger	1 8-ounce can pineapple
2 green onions, cut in	chunks
small pieces	1 tablespoon cornstarch
3 tablespoons soy sauce	

With a sharp cleaver, cut the chicken into 2-inch pieces,
bone and all, or have the butcher do it. Heat the oil to
365°. Fry the chicken in it until browned. Drain. Put
chicken pieces in a bowl and add the ginger root, green
onion, soy sauce, sugar, sherry and salt. Place bowl on a
rack in a pan of boiling water. Cover and steam 40 minutes
or until tender.

Drain syrup from canned pineapple and combine syrup
with juices from steamed chicken. Heat. Add pineapple
chunks and blend in cornstarch until thickened. Arrange
chicken on a serving dish and pour sauce over it.

◖ SERVES 3–4.

Cantonese Fried Chicken

3-pound frying chicken,   2 tablespoons soy sauce
    disjointed   3 tablespoons gin
1 clove garlic, minced   ½ cup sifted cornstarch
1 teaspoon sugar   vegetable oil for deep frying

Cut the chicken breast in four pieces. Wash and dry all
the chicken pieces and rub with the combined garlic,
sugar, soy sauce and gin. Let stand 15 minutes. Roll in
the cornstarch and fry in hot (360°) oil until golden
brown. Drain. Place in a skillet, cover and cook over low
heat 15 minutes, or until tender.
(SERVES 4–6.

Fried Chicken, Peking Style

3 tablespoons dry sherry   1 tablespoon sesame-seed
1 teaspoon ground ginger   or vegetable oil
8 tablespoons soy sauce   2 teaspoons sugar
2 green onions, chopped   1 teaspoon minced ginger
3-pound frying chicken,   root or ½ teaspoon
    disjointed   ground ginger
vegetable oil for deep frying ½ teaspoon minced
1½ tablespoons cider   garlic
    vinegar

Combine the sherry, ginger, 5 tablespoons soy sauce and
1 chopped green onion. Add the chicken pieces and marinate 1 hour. Heat the oil to 365° and fry the chicken
until browned. Drain and cut into small pieces. Arrange
on a serving dish and keep hot. Combine the remaining
soy sauce, vinegar, sesame-seed oil, sugar, ginger root or
ground ginger, and garlic. Mix well, heat and pour over

chicken before serving. Sprinkle with the remaining green onion.

❲ SERVES 3–4.

Steamed Fried Chicken

3½-pound frying chicken, quartered

2 tablespoons soy sauce

2 tablespoons dry sherry

2 green onions, sliced

3 slices ginger root or ¾ teaspoon ground ginger

3 tablespoons flour

½ teaspoon salt

1 egg

vegetable oil for deep frying

Put the chicken, soy sauce, sherry, green onions and ginger in a bowl. Place bowl on a rack in a saucepan and add boiling water to reach the rack. Cover the pan and cook 30 minutes, or until chicken is tender. Remove chicken and reserve juices. Bone chicken and let stand until cold. Combine the flour, salt, egg and a little of the reserved juices to make a paste. Coat chicken with the paste and fry in 370° oil until light brown and crisp. Drain. Serve hot.

❲ SERVES 3–4.

Fried Chicken with Green Peppers

2 whole raw chicken breasts, boned and cubed

4 tablespoons dry sherry

4 teaspoons corn-starch

1 egg white

½ cup vegetable oil

9 small green peppers, seeded and cut in small squares

2 teaspoons salt

½ teaspoon sugar

½ teaspoon monosodium glutamate

Combine the chicken cubes, 1 tablespoon sherry, the corn-starch and unbeaten egg white. Heat 5 tablespoons oil in a skillet and sauté chicken until it turns golden brown. Drain. Pour oil from skillet and wipe clean. Add remaining oil, heat and sauté green peppers 3 minutes, stirring frequently. Replace chicken in the skillet with the remaining sherry, the salt, sugar and monosodium glutamate. Mix well. Cook 2 minutes more.

《 SERVES 4–6.

Fried Chicken with Brown Sauce

4 *Chinese dried mushrooms*	2¼ *cups vegetable oil*
2 *whole raw chicken breasts, boned and cut in small cubes*	2 *bamboo shoots, cut in small cubes*
2 *tablespoons cornstarch*	¼ *teaspoon dried ground red chili peppers*
2 *tablespoons dry sherry*	4 *tablespoons* chiang *(bottled Chinese brown sauce)*
1 *teaspoon salt*	

Soak the mushrooms in warm water 10 minutes. Drain and dice. Toss the chicken cubes with the cornstarch, sherry and salt. Heat 2 cups oil in a skillet until it bubbles. Fry the chicken in it until browned. Drain. Heat the remaining ¼ cup oil in a skillet and sauté the mushrooms, bamboo shoots and red peppers 2 minutes. Stir in *chiang*. Add the chicken; mix well. Cook 2 minutes more. Serve hot.

《 SERVES 4–6.

Spicy Barbecued Chicken

4 *pound roasting chicken*	½ *teaspoon ground cloves*
2 *cloves garlic, minced*	½ *teaspoon cinnamon*
2 *teaspoons salt*	½ *teaspoon anise*
¼ *teaspoon black pepper*	¼ *cup soy sauce*
1 *teaspoon sugar*	2 *tablespoons vegetable oil*

Wash and dry the whole chicken. Rub inside and out with the combined garlic, salt, pepper, sugar, cloves, cinnamon, anise, soy sauce and oil. Let stand 1 hour. Put the chicken on a rack in a shallow roasting pan and roast in a 425° oven 2 hours, or until tender and browned, basting and turning frequently. To serve, disjoint or chop with meat cleaver into inch-wide pieces.

❲ SERVES 4–6.

Walnut Chicken

2 *whole raw chicken breasts*
¼ *cup soy sauce*
3 *tablespoons dry sherry*
2 *teaspoons sugar*
1 *teaspoon salt*
3 *tablespoons cornstarch*

2 *cups vegetable oil*
2 *cups blanched walnuts*
1 *cup cubed bamboo shoots*
1 *cup sliced green onion*
½ *cup diced water chestnuts*
¼ *cup chicken broth*

Remove the skin and bones and cut the chicken breasts in small cubes. Toss in a mixture of the soy sauce, sherry, sugar, salt and cornstarch. Heat the oil in a skillet; fry the walnuts in it until browned. Drain, reserving ⅓ cup oil. Heat 3 tablespoons oil in the skillet; sauté the bamboo shoots, green onion and water chestnuts 3 minutes, stirring frequently. Remove from pan.

Heat the remaining 3 tablespoons oil in the skillet; cook the chicken in it until browned, stirring frequently. Add the broth; cook over low heat 5 minutes. Return the vegetables and walnuts. Heat and serve.

❲ SERVES 4–6.

Chicken and Almonds

2 whole raw chicken
breasts
⅓ cup vegetable oil
½ cup blanched almonds
¾ cup sliced green onion
1 cup sliced celery
1 pound snow peas or 1
package frozen

1 4-ounce can button
mushrooms, drained
3 tablespoons soy sauce
1 10½-ounce can chicken
broth
1½ tablespoons cornstarch

Remove the skin and bones from the chicken breasts and dice the chicken. Heat the oil in a skillet; brown the almonds in it. Remove almonds with a slotted spoon and drain on paper towels. In the oil remaining in the skillet, cook the chicken 3 minutes, stirring constantly. Add the green onion, celery, snow peas, mushrooms and soy sauce. Cook 2 minutes, still stirring. Add 1 cup of the broth; bring to a boil and cook over medium heat 5 minutes.

Mix the cornstarch with the remaining broth, add to the skillet and stir until sauce is thickened. Mix in the almonds and serve.

◖ SERVES 4–6.

Brown Chicken

3½ pound fryer
1 teaspoon salt
¼ teaspoon black pepper
2¼ cups vegetable oil
¼ cup soy sauce
1 cup chicken broth

1 tablespoon dry sherry
¼ cup sliced green onion
¼ cup diced water chestnuts
1 tablespoon cornstarch
¼ cup cold water

With a sharp cleaver, chop the chicken into small pieces, bone and all, or have the butcher do it. Mix together the salt, pepper, 2 tablespoons oil and 2 tablespoons soy sauce. Toss the chicken pieces in the mixture and let stand 15 minutes. Heat the remaining oil in a skillet; brown the chicken in it. Drain chicken. Pour off all but 3 tablespoons of the oil from the skillet. Add the broth, sherry, green onion, water chestnuts and remaining soy sauce. Bring to a boil and return the chicken. Cover and cook over low heat 15 minutes. Remove the chicken, arrange on a serving dish and keep hot. Mix the cornstarch with the water. Stir into the liquid in the skillet. Cook over low heat, stirring steadily until thickened. Pour over the chicken.

《 SERVES 4–6.

Steamed Chicken and Rice

4 *pound chicken,*	1 *slice ginger root or ½*
cut up	*teaspoon ground ginger*
6 *cups water*	¼ *cup dry sherry*
1 *cup sliced onion*	1 *cup raw long-grain rice*
2 *teaspoons salt*	6 *tablespoons soy sauce*

Wash the chicken and put in a saucepan with the water and onion. Bring to a boil. Add the salt, ginger and sherry; cover and cook over low heat 45 minutes or until chicken is tender. Remove the chicken from the stock; discard the bones and then cut chicken into small cubes. Add the rice to the stock; cover and cook 30 minutes. Return the chicken, heat, and serve in deep bowls, with a tablespoon of soy sauce in each. The dish will be like a thick stew.

《 SERVES 6.

Crisp Soy Chicken

3 *pound fryer*	2 *tablespoons dry sherry*
3 *cups boiling water*	¼ *cup flour*
½ *cup soy sauce*	2 *teaspoons salt*
½ *cup honey*	1 *quart vegetable oil*
¼ *cup cider vinegar*	

Have the chicken left whole. Clean and wash. Cook in the boiling water 30 minutes. Drain, rinse under cold water and dry carefully inside and out. Don't tear the skin.

Mix together the soy sauce, honey, vinegar and sherry. Brush the skin with the mixture and let stand 30 minutes, or until dry. Brush again with the soy mixture, then sprinkle with the flour and salt. Let stand until dry. Heat the oil to 380°. Lower the chicken into it. Fry until browned and crisp. The skin may be removed and served as an appetizer sandwich with Chinese Bread (see page 73) with green onions, duck sauce and mustard, and the chicken itself cut up into small pieces as a main course. Or leave the skin on and cut chicken into serving-sized pieces.

❴ SERVES 4–6.

Chicken Balls

2 whole raw chicken breasts	¼ teaspoon white pepper
1 10½-ounce can chicken broth	2 tablespoons cornstarch
	5 egg whites
1½ teaspoons salt	vegetable oil for deep frying
½ teaspoon monosodium glutamate	2 tablespoons dry sherry
	3 slices bacon, fried and crumbled

Remove the skin and bones and chop the chicken breasts very fine, adding ¼ cup of broth gradually while chopping. Mix in the salt, monosodium glutamate, pepper, 1 tablespoon cornstarch and 4 tablespoons of the unbeaten egg whites. Beat the remaining egg whites until stiff and fold into the chicken mixture. Heat the oil to 370°. Drop the mixture into it by the heaping teaspoon. Fry until browned. Drain and keep hot. In a saucepan, mix the remaining cornstarch with the sherry. Add the remaining broth. Cook over medium heat, stirring steadily until thickened. Add the chicken balls; cook 3 minutes. Turn into a bowl and sprinkle with the bacon.

❘[SERVES 4.

Minced Chicken

6 Chinese dried mush-
  rooms
1 whole chicken breast
2 tablespoons cornstarch
2 tablespoons dry sherry
3 tablespoons vegetable oil
¼ cup chopped celery

¼ cup chopped bamboo
  shoots or water chestnuts
½ teaspoon salt
½ teaspoon sugar
2 teaspoons soy sauce
¾ cup chicken broth
lettuce leaves

Wash the mushrooms, cover with warm water and let soak 10 minutes. Drain and chop. Remove the skin and bones and chop the chicken breast. Toss with 1 table-spoon cornstarch and the sherry. Heat the oil in a skillet; sauté the mixture 5 minutes, stirring frequently. Mix in the mushrooms, celery, bamboo shoots or water chestnuts, salt, sugar and soy sauce. Cook over low heat 5 minutes. Mix the remaining cornstarch with the chicken broth. Add to the chicken mixture, stirring steadily until thickened. Serve in lettuce cups.

❘[SERVES 4–6.

Chicken Pancakes, Cantonese Style

½ cup chopped canned
  mushrooms, drained
2 tablespoons chopped
  green onion
1 teaspoon soy sauce
¼ teaspoon black pepper

2 tablespoons flour
5 eggs
1 cup diced cooked chicken
½ cup diced water chest-
  nuts, well drained
¼ cup vegetable oil

Combine all of the ingredients, except the oil, in the bowl of an electric blender. Cover and blend at high speed until smooth. Or beat the eggs in a bowl, then add the remaining ingredients, all finely chopped. Heat the oil in a skillet; drop the mixture into it by the heaping tablespoon. Cook until browned on both sides. Serve with strong Chinese or English mustard and ketchup.

⟮ SERVES 3–4.

Skewered Chicken

1 *large boned breast of chicken, cut into pieces 1 inch wide, 1½ inches long and ¼-inch thick*

15 *water chestnuts, thinly sliced*

1 *clove garlic, pressed*

2 *slices ginger, chopped, or ½ teaspoon ground ginger*

1 *teaspoon Hoisin sauce*

⅓ *cup soy sauce*

1 *teaspoon sugar*

¼ *cup dry sherry*

⅛ *teaspoon monosodium glutamate*

1 *tablespoon oil*

¼ *pound sliced bacon, cut in 1-inch lengths*

Marinate the chicken and water chestnuts in a marinade made of the remaining ingredients listed above (except the bacon) for 2 hours or more in the refrigerator. Thread each skewer alternately with pieces of chicken, bacon, and water chestnuts. Broil 5 minutes in the oven or on a spit. Remove to a warm plate. Serve hot with rice.

⟮ SERVES 4.

Chicken and Ham with Oyster Sauce

2 whole raw chicken breasts

2¼ teaspoons salt

½ teaspoon ground ginger

3 tablespoons dry sherry

¼ teaspoon monosodium glutamate

20 thin slices cooked ham, 1 inch wide and 2 inches long

3 tablespoons peanut or vegetable oil

1 slice ginger root or ¼ teaspoon ground ginger

½ pound broccoli, cut in pieces 2 inches long, ½-inch thick

½ clove garlic, crushed

1 cup chicken broth

2 tablespoons oyster sauce

1 teaspoon soy sauce

⅛ teaspoon black pepper

½ teaspoon sugar

2 teaspoons cornstarch mixed with 2 teaspoons water

Rub the chicken breasts with a mixture of 1½ teaspoons salt, ½ teaspoon ginger, 1 tablespoon sherry and the monosodium glutamate. Arrange the breasts, skin side down, in a deep, glass baking dish placed in a covered 12-inch frying pan to which 2 cups boiling water has been added and steam 20 minutes. Bone breasts and cut them into pieces 1 inch by 2 inches. Arrange alternately with the ham slices on a platter, cover with foil, and keep warm.

Heat 2 tablespoons oil in a frying pan, add the ginger slice, ½ teaspoon salt and the broccoli, and sauté 2 minutes. Add the remaining 2 tablespoons sherry and ¼ cup water, cover and cook 3 minutes. Drain broccoli and arrange around the chicken and ham slices.

To make the sauce, heat 1 tablespoon oil in a frying pan. Add the garlic, chicken broth, the remaining ¼ teaspoon salt, the oyster sauce, soy sauce, pepper and sugar and bring to a boil. Thicken with the cornstarch paste. Heat and pour over the chicken-and-ham platter.

⟨ SERVES 6.

Chicken Salad

¼ cup sesame seeds

2 tablespoons vegetable oil

3 tablespoons cider vinegar

2 tablespoons soy sauce

¼ teaspoon Tabasco

1 teaspoon sugar

½ teaspoon ground ginger

2 cucumbers

2 cups julienne-cut cooked chicken

½ cup thinly sliced green onion

Brown the sesame seeds in a skillet. Shake the pan frequently to keep them from burning. Pound the browned sesame seeds or put through a Mouli grater. Mix the ground sesame seeds with the oil, vinegar, soy sauce, Tabasco, sugar and ginger. Peel the cucumbers, cut in sixths lengthwise, then, holding the lengths together so that the cucumber retains its original shape, slice paper thin. Toss with the chicken and green onion. Arrange on a serving dish and pour dressing over it.

(SERVES 4–6.

Cold Marinated Chicken

3 pound chicken

1 tablespoon salt

2 slices ginger root or ½ teaspoon ground ginger

2 green onions, sliced

1½ cups water

¼ cup soy sauce

½ cup dry sherry

Wash and dry the chicken and rub with the salt. Put the ginger and green onions in interior of chicken. Put chicken in a saucepan with the water. Cover, bring to a boil and cook over low heat 45 minutes or until tender. Add small amounts of boiling water if required. Drain. Combine the soy sauce and sherry and pour over the chicken. Marinate in the refrigerator over night, turning the chicken a few times. Slice and serve cold.

(SERVES 3–4.

Glazed Roast Duck

4–5-*pound duck*
⅓ *cup chopped onion*
⅓ *cup chopped celery*
2 *tablespoons dry sherry*
2 *teaspoons sugar*
½ *teaspoon anise*

½ *teaspoon cinnamon*
½ *cup soy sauce*
1 *tablespoon salt*
¼ *cup honey*
2 *tablespoons cider vinegar*

Remove as much fat as possible from the duck. Tie the neck opening securely. Put the onion, celery, sherry, sugar, anise, cinnamon and all but 1 tablespoon of the soy sauce in a saucepan. Bring to a boil. Pour into the interior of the duck and sew up the opening. Rub duck with salt. Arrange on a rack in a shallow roasting pan and roast in a 475° oven 30 minutes. Pour off fat. Brush duck with the combined honey, vinegar and remaining 1 tablespoon soy sauce. Reduce heat to 400° and roast 2½ hours, brushing every 30 minutes with the vinegar-honey mixture.

To serve, snip the threads at opening and drain (use liquid as a sauce for the duck), and cut the duck in small pieces.

◖ SERVES 4–6.

Duck, Szechwan Style

4–4½-*pound duck*
4 *teaspoons salt*
4 *peppercorns, crushed*
1 *teaspoon five-spice powder*
2 *tablespoons dry sherry*
¼ *teaspoon monosodium glutamate*

2 *slices ginger root or* ½
teaspoon ground ginger
2 *green onions, chopped*
flour
1 *egg, beaten*
bread crumbs
vegetable oil for deep frying

Rub the duck with 1 teaspoon salt, let stand 20 minutes and rinse in cold water. Dry with paper towels. Rub the skin with a mixture of 1½ teaspoons salt, the peppercorns, five-spice powder, 1 tablespoon sherry and the monosodium glutamate. In the cavity of the duck put a mixture of ginger, green onions, the remaining 1 tablespoon sherry and 1½ teaspoons salt. Put the duck in a plastic bag and place in the refrigerator for at least 4–5 hours, and preferably overnight.

To cook, remove duck from plastic bag, place in a pan and cover with foil. Steam on a rack in a large covered pot containing 2 inches of boiling water for 1 hour over medium-low heat. Remove from pan, drain and dry carefully (do not break the skin). Place in the refrigerator long enough for it to become thoroughly chilled. Then coat first with flour and then with beaten egg. Roll in bread crumbs and fry in deep hot (375°) oil until golden brown. To serve, disjoint the duck or cut it into ½-inch segments. Serve hot, garnished with lemon slices.

◖ SERVES 6.

Pungent Fried Duck

4 *pound duck, disjointed*
3 *tablespoons cornstarch*
3 *tablespoons flour*
1 *teaspoon salt*
¼ *teaspoon black pepper*
3 *tablespoons vegetable oil*
2 *cups thinly sliced green onion*
2 *cloves garlic, minced*

1 *tablespoon minced ginger root or 1 teaspoon ground ginger*
4 *tablespoons gin*
4 *tablespoons soy sauce*
½ *cup chicken broth*
½ *teaspoon monosodium glutamate*

Wash and dry duck pieces. Remove as much fat as possible. Combine the cornstarch, flour, salt and pepper.

Roll the duck in the mixture. Heat the oil in a deep skillet and brown the duck all over. Pour off the fat. Add the green onion, garlic and ginger and cook 2 minutes, stirring frequently. Mix in the gin, soy sauce, broth and monosodium glutamate. Cover and cook over low heat 1 hour or until liquid is absorbed and duck tender.

❰ SERVES 4–6.

Spicy Fried Duck

4–5-pound duck
4 tablespoons dry sherry
1½ tablespoons salt
2 teaspoons sugar
½ teaspoon dried ground red chili peppers
1 green onion, chopped
6 slices ginger root or ¾ teaspoon ground ginger
6 star anise or 1 teaspoon ground anise
5 tablespoons flour
2 eggs, lightly beaten
vegetable oil for deep frying

Rub the duck with the sherry and let stand 30 minutes. Rub duck with a mixture of the salt, sugar and ground chili peppers. Place in a large bowl, with the green onion, ginger root and anise on top of the duck. Place bowl on a rack in a large saucepan. Add boiling water to reach rack, cover saucepan and steam for 1¼ hours, or until duck is tender. Remove duck and cool. Add the flour to the beaten eggs and mix well; coat duck with mixture. Heat the oil to 365° and fry duck until crisp and brown, about 15 minutes. Drain. Cut into small pieces. Serve hot with two dishes of condiments (for each person) for dipping—one dish containing 2 tablespoons ketchup, the other a combination of 2 teaspoons salt and 2 teaspoons coarsely cracked black pepper.

❰ SERVES 4–6.

Crisp Fried Duck

4–5-pound duck
2 cups soy
  sauce
4 cloves garlic

3 tablespoons minced ginger
  root or 1 tablespoon
  ground ginger
vegetable oil for deep frying

Wash and dry the whole duck, removing any excess fat.
In a deep saucepan, combine the duck, soy sauce, garlic,
ginger and enough water to barely cover. Bring to a boil,
cover and cook over low heat 1 hour or until duck is
tender. Drain, dry and cool the duck.

Heat the oil to 370°. Carefully lower the duck into it.
Fry until browned and crisp, turning the duck if necessary
to brown all sides. Drain and cut into small pieces, bone
and all.

❆ SERVES 4–6.

Pressed Duck

This is a fairly complicated recipe, but worth the effort.
Begin the preparation the day before you want to serve it.

4–5-pound duck
boiling water
1 onion, sliced
1 stalk celery, sliced
1 bay leaf
2 tablespoons soy sauce

2 teaspoons salt
¾ teaspoon black pepper
1 tablespoon flour
1 tablespoon cornstarch
1 teaspoon sugar
1 egg, beaten

Wash the duck, place in a deep saucepan and cover with
boiling water. Simmer 30 minutes; add the onion, celery,
bay leaf and soy sauce. Cook 1 hour longer, or until tender,
turning the duck once or twice. Drain, reserving 1 cup
of stock. Cool, then carefully remove the skin of the duck,
keeping the pieces of skin as large as possible. Cut the

meat of the duck in small pieces. Put the skin, outside
edge down, on the bottom of a square pan, sprinkle with
1 teaspoon salt, ¼ teaspoon pepper and the flour. Toss
the duck meat with the cornstarch, sugar and remaining
salt and pepper. Spread on the skin about ½-inch thick.
Press down with a heavy pan or other weight. Remove
weight and brush top with the egg. Cover with foil or
waxed paper and again weight it down. Chill overnight.

BATTER

½ teaspoon salt · 1 egg
vegetable oil for deep frying · 2 tablespoons water
¼ cup flour

Cut the pressed duck in 1-inch squares. Beat the egg and
water; stir in the flour and salt until smooth. Dip the duck
pieces in this batter. Heat the oil to 375° and fry the
squares in it until brown and crisp. Drain and keep hot.

SAUCE

1 cup reserved stock · 1 tablespoon molasses
1 tablespoon corn- · ¼ cup minced green onion
starch · ¼ cup slivered toasted
1 tablespoon soy sauce · almonds

Mix the stock, cornstarch, soy sauce and molasses together
in a saucepan. Cook over medium heat, stirring constantly,
until thickened and clear. Pour the sauce into a serving
dish, arrange duck squares over it and sprinkle with the
green onion and almonds.

⟨ SERVES 4–6.

Fried Pigeon

2 *pigeons or squabs*   1 *teaspoon salt*
1 *teaspoon coarsely ground*   4 *tablespoons honey*
  black pepper   *vegetable oil for deep frying*
2 *tablespoons soy sauce*

Wash and dry the birds. Rub inside and out with a
mixture of the pepper, soy sauce and salt. Brush the skin
with honey. Heat the oil to 360° and fry the birds until
brown and tender. Cut into small pieces and serve.

❮ SERVES 2–4.

Skewered Chicken Livers

18 *chicken livers*   ½ *cup soy sauce*
18 *slices bacon*   3 *tablespoons honey*
½ *pound boneless pork*   ¼ *cup dry sherry*
12 *water chestnuts, cut*   1 *teaspoon salt*
   in half   ½ *teaspoon black pepper*

Wash the livers, removing any discolored areas. Cut each
liver in half. Cut the bacon in half crosswise. Wrap a
half piece around each piece of liver. Cut the pork in
24 paper-thin slices, the same size as the livers. Using
12 skewers, thread the livers, pork and water chestnuts
on them, starting and ending with the livers. Mix together
the soy sauce, honey, sherry, salt and pepper. Marinate the
skewers in this mixture for 30 minutes, basting and turning frequently. Drain; arrange on a shallow baking pan.
Bake in a 350° oven 20 minutes, turning the skewers to
brown all sides.

❮ SERVES 12.

Sweet-and-Sour Chicken Livers

1 *pound chicken livers*
2 *stalks celery*
1 *carrot*
1 *cucumber*
1 *tablespoon cornstarch*
3 *tablespoons sugar*
½ *cup tarragon vinegar*
¼ *cup water*
1 *tablespoon soy sauce*

2 *tablespoons*
  vegetable oil
1 *clove garlic, minced*
2 *teaspoons minced ginger*
  root or ½ teaspoon
  ground ginger
1½ *teaspoons salt*
¼ *teaspoon black pepper*

Wash the livers. Cut them in half, cover with boiling water and soak 10 minutes. Drain and dry. Slice the celery diagonally. Cut the carrot in julienne strips. Halve the cucumber lengthwise, remove seeds, and cut in ½-inch pieces. Combine the cornstarch, sugar, vinegar, water and soy sauce. Heat the oil in a skillet and sauté the livers, garlic and ginger root 4 minutes. Stir in the salt, pepper, vinegar mixture, celery, carrot and cucumber. Cook, stirring, until thickened, then cover and cook over low heat 5 minutes.

⟨ SERVES 4–6.

Vegetables

8

Vegetables

Growing Your Own Bean Sprouts

Mung peas are small greenish-colored peas which may be purchased in Chinese or Japanese food shops.

Wash the peas and soak in warm water overnight (1 cup peas to 6 cups water). Drain well. Put the peas in separate layers on wet paper towels in a colander; the top layer of peas should be covered by a wet towel. Keep in a dark place at room temperature for 3 or 4 days, sprinkling twice daily with lukewarm water to thoroughly wet the towels and peas. Keep a container under the colander to catch the water that drains through the colander. At the end of the soaking time, when the peas have sprouted, remove the sprouts from towels, rinse under cold water to remove the husks, and use as directed in the recipes.

1 cup of mung peas will make about 1 pound of bean sprouts.

Peking Bean Sprouts

3 tablespoons vegetable oil
1 can bean sprouts, drained
2 teaspoons sliced ginger
    root or 1 teaspoon ground
    ginger
½ teaspoon salt
4 green onions, sliced
2 tablespoons soy
    sauce

Heat the oil in a skillet and sauté the bean sprouts 1 minute, stirring steadily. Mix in the ginger and salt, cover and cook 2 minutes. Stir in the green onions and soy sauce and cook 3 minutes.

❬ SERVES 3–4.

Fried Bean Sprouts with Green Peppers

1 pound fresh bean
    sprouts
5 tablespoons oil
1½ cups chopped green
    pepper
2 tablespoons dry sherry
1 teaspoon salt
¼ teaspoon monosodium
    glutamate

Remove the ends of fresh bean sprouts and soak in cold water 10 minutes. Drain well. Heat the oil and sauté the bean sprouts and green pepper 5 minutes. Mix in the sherry, salt and monosodium glutamate; cook 1 minute, stirring constantly.

❬ SERVES 4–6.

Note: If canned bean sprouts are substituted, they need only to be drained.

Fried Spinach

2 pounds fresh spinach
    or 2 packages chopped
    frozen, thawed
3 tablespoons vegetable oil
1 teaspoon salt

Thoroughly wash the fresh spinach and drain well. Chop coarsely; or drain chopped frozen spinach. Heat the oil in a skillet, add the spinach and salt and cook over high heat, stirring constantly, for 4 minutes.

◖ SERVES 2–4.

Braised Bamboo Shoots

6 *Chinese dried mushrooms* ¼ *cup water*
4 *tablespoons vegetable oil* 2 *tablespoons sugar*
3 *cups cubed bamboo shoots* 1 *tablespoon dry sherry*
3 *tablespoons soy sauce*

Soak the mushrooms in hot water for 30 minutes. Drain and slice. Heat the oil in a skillet; add the mushrooms and bamboo shoots. Cook over medium heat 5 minutes. Add the soy sauce, water, sugar and sherry. Cover and cook 15 minutes.

◖ SERVES 4–6.

Bamboo Shoots with Chili Sauce

1 *29-ounce can bamboo* ¼ *cup chili sauce*
  shoots 1 *tablespoon soy sauce*
2 *cups vegetable oil* 1 *teaspoon sugar*

Drain the bamboo shoots and cut in matchlike strips. Dry on paper towels. Heat the oil in a skillet; fry the bamboo shoots until golden brown. Remove with a slotted spoon. Pour off all but 2 tablespoons oil. Mix in the chili sauce, soy sauce and sugar. Bring to a boil and return the bamboo shoots. Mix until bamboo shoots are hot and coated with the sauce.

◖ SERVES 4–6.

Sautéed Lettuce

1 head romaine	½ teaspoon salt
⅓ cup vegetable oil	1 teaspoon monosodium
1 clove garlic, minced	glutamate

Wash and dry the romaine. Discard the large outer leaves and separate the rest of the lettuce. Heat the oil in a deep skillet; lightly brown the garlic in it, then add the lettuce, salt and monosodium glutamate. Cook over medium heat 5 minutes, stirring frequently.

❲ SERVES 2–4.

Stuffed Cucumbers

8 cucumbers	3 tablespoons soy sauce
½ pound ground pork	3 tablespoons cornstarch
1 teaspoon salt	3 tablespoons vegetable oil
½ teaspoon ground ginger	1 cup beef broth
¼ cup chopped green onion	½ cup water
¼ cup diced celery	

Lightly pare the cucumbers. Cut in half lengthwise, then in thirds crosswise. Scoop out the seeds. Mix together the pork, salt, ginger, green onion, celery, 1 tablespoon soy sauce, 1 tablespoon cornstarch and 1 tablespoon oil. Stuff the cucumbers with the mixture.

Heat the remaining oil in a skillet; arrange the cucumbers in it, stuffed side up. Add the broth and water. Cover, bring to a boil and cook over medium heat 35 minutes, or until no pink remains in the pork.

In a saucepan, mix the remaining cornstarch and soy sauce with the water. Cook, stirring constantly until thickened. Arrange the cucumbers on a serving dish and pour the sauce over them.

❲ SERVES 6–8.

Stuffed Eggplant

1 large eggplant
8 water chest-
  nuts
¾ pound ground pork
  (or beef)
1 small onion,
  minced

1 tablespoon minced fresh
  ginger or 1 teaspoon
  ground
1 tablespoon dry sherry
2 teaspoons soy sauce
½ teaspoon salt
1 teaspoon sugar

Wash and peel the eggplant, cut in half lengthwise and remove the seeds. Mince the water chestnuts and combine with the pork, onion, ginger, sherry, soy sauce, salt, and sugar. Mix well. Stuff each half of the eggplant with the mixture. Steam 30 minutes.

❲ SERVES 2.

Stuffed Green Peppers

14 medium-sized green
  peppers
10 water chestnuts
¼ cup chopped green onion
1 tablespoon dry sherry
1 teaspoon cornstarch

½ teaspoon salt
3 tablespoons soy sauce
1 teaspoon sugar
1 tablespoon vegetable oil
1 cup ground pork

Cut the peppers into halves crosswise and remove seeds. Bring to a boil in 3 cups water and then simmer 5 minutes. Remove, drain and set aside. Chop the water chestnuts and combine with the green onion, sherry, cornstarch, salt, soy sauce, sugar, oil and pork and mix well. Stuff each pepper half with the mixture. Arrange in a large bowl and place the bowl, covered, in a pan of hot water. Steam 40 minutes.

❲ SERVES 8.

Stuffed Mushrooms

12 medium-sized Chinese
   dried mushrooms (or
   fresh, if you prefer)
 6 water chestnuts
½ pound ground pork
½ cup minced cooked ham
½ teaspoon salt

½ tablespoon cornstarch
 2 tablespoons soy sauce
 1 egg white
 3 tablespoons vegetable oil
 1 tablespoon sugar
 1 tablespoon sherry
 2 tablespoons chicken stock

Soak the dried mushrooms in warm water to cover until
they expand. Wash well and remove the stems and any
foreign particles. Soak in second water 15 minutes. Squeeze
dry. Fresh mushrooms need only to be rinsed in cold
water and dried on paper towels. Mince the water chestnuts and combine with the pork, ham, salt, cornstarch
and 1 tablespoon soy sauce. Add the egg white and mix
well. Heat the oil in a skillet, add the mushrooms and
sauté 2 minutes. Add the sugar, sherry, and the remaining
1 tablespoon soy sauce and sauté 1 minute longer. Pack
the stuffing mixture into each inverted mushroom. Arrange
in a large bowl and place the bowl, covered, in a pan of
hot water. Steam 30 minutes. Sprinkle with 2 tablespoons
hot chicken stock.

❬ SERVES 4.

Mixed Vegetables

 1 pound Chinese celery
   cabbage
½ pound bean sprouts,
   fresh or canned
 3 tablespoons vegetable oil
 3 bamboo shoots, sliced
½ pound snow peas, or 1
   package frozen

 6 water chestnuts,
   sliced
 1 teaspoon salt
¼ teaspoon monosodium
   glutamate
½ teaspoon sugar
¼ cup water

Wash the celery cabbage and slice thin, diagonally. (If not available, use celery or cabbage.) Wash the fresh sprouts, or drain the canned ones. Heat the oil in a large skillet. Add the celery cabbage, bean sprouts, bamboo shoots, snow peas, water chestnuts, salt, monosodium glutamate and sugar. Cook over high heat 1 minute, stirring constantly. Add the water; cover and cook 3 minutes. The vegetables should be crisp.

 ❲ SERVES 4–6.

Creamed Celery Cabbage

3 tablespoons peanut or vegetable oil

1 slice ginger root or ⅛ teaspoon ground ginger

½ teaspoon salt

1 pound celery cabbage, cut in pieces ½-inch wide and 2½ inches long

½ cup chicken broth

⅛ teaspoon black pepper

⅛ teaspoon monosodium glutamate

2 teaspoons cornstarch mixed with ½ cup milk

1 tablespoon chopped cooked ham

Heat the oil in a frying pan. Add the ginger, salt, and celery cabbage and sauté 2 minutes. Add the chicken broth, cover, and cook 3 minutes longer over low heat. (If you have used sliced ginger, remove the slice at this point.) Add the pepper and monosodium glutamate and thicken with the cornstarch paste. Cook 1 minute longer. Remove to a serving dish and sprinkle with chopped ham.

 ❲ SERVES 4.

Sesame Sweet-Potato Balls

1 16-ounce can mashed sweet potatoes	¼ cup flour
⅔ cup sugar	½ cup water
½ teaspoon ground ginger	1 cup sesame seeds
2 egg yolks	vegetable oil for deep frying

Be sure the sweet potatoes are mashed very smooth. Beat in the sugar, ginger and egg yolks until fluffy. Form tablespoons of the mixture into balls. Mix the flour and water until smooth. Roll the balls in the mixture, then in the sesame seeds. Heat the oil to 375°. Fry the balls in it until delicately browned. Drain and serve hot.

⟦ SERVES 6–8.

Potato Pancakes, Chinese Style

4 cups seasoned mashed potatoes	¼ cup chopped cooked ham (optional)
4 strips broiled bacon, crumbled	1 egg, beaten
	flour
2 green onions, chopped	6 tablespoons peanut or vegetable oil

Mix together the mashed potatoes, crumbled bacon, green onions and chopped ham and shape into 3-inch rounds ½-inch thick. Dip first into the beaten egg and then into flour. Shake to remove the excess flour. Heat 4 tablespoons oil in a skillet and sauté the cakes over medium heat until golden brown on both sides. Add the remaining 2 tablespoons oil from time to time if necessary to prevent sticking. Serve with Chinese Mustard.

⟦ MAKES 8 CAKES, SERVES 4.

Asparagus with Chicken Broth

2 tablespoons vegetable oil
½ cup chicken broth
1 tablespoon dry sherry
½ teaspoon salt
2 tablespoons soy sauce
1 tablespoon cornstarch
    mixed with 1 teaspoon
    water
16 stalks cooked asparagus

Heat a large skillet and add the oil. Add chicken broth, sherry, salt, soy sauce and the mixture of cornstarch and water. Cook 1 minute, stirring to blend well. Add the asparagus and simmer 3 minutes.

⟨ SERVES 4.

Asparagus with Ginger-Sherry Sauce

1½ teaspoons salt
12 fresh asparagus spears,
    cut in ½-inch pieces
1 tablespoon
    vegetable oil
1 slice ginger root or ⅛
    teaspoon ground ginger
1 tablespoon sherry
⅛ teaspoon monosodium
    glutamate

Add 1¼ teaspoons salt to 4 cups water in a saucepan and bring to a boil. Add the asparagus and bring back to a boil for 1 minute. Drain and remove to a heated dish. In a frying pan heat the oil until very hot and add the ginger, sherry, the remaining salt and the monosodium glutamate. Cook 1 minute, stirring constantly. Pour over asparagus.

⟨ SERVES 4.

Asparagus with Crab Sauce

1½ teaspoons salt
12 fresh asparagus spears,
   cut in ½-inch pieces
½ cup chicken broth
⅛ teaspoon white pepper
⅛ teaspoon monosodium
   glutamate

1 teaspoon cornstarch
   mixed with 2 teaspoons
   water
½ cup crabmeat, fresh or
   frozen
1 egg white, beaten stiff
   but not dry

Add 1¼ teaspoons salt to 4 cups water in a saucepan and
bring to a boil. Add the asparagus and bring to a boil for
1 minute. Drain and remove to a heated dish.

Bring the broth to a boil and add the pepper and monosodium glutamate. Gradually thicken with the cornstarch
paste and then add the crabmeat. Remove from heat as
soon as the crabmeat is hot and then slowly add the
beaten egg white, folding it in gently. Pour the sauce
over the asparagus.

❨ SERVES 4.

Broccoli with Oyster Sauce

1 pound broccoli
½ teaspoon salt
4 tablespoons
   vegetable oil

2 tablespoons oyster sauce
   mixed with 1 teaspoon
   sugar and ⅓ cup of the
   broccoli cooking liquid

Wash the broccoli, peel the stems, and slice diagonally.
Bring 2 cups water to a boil, add salt and broccoli and
simmer 2 minutes. Drain, saving ⅓ cup of the liquid.
Put the oil in a hot skillet, add the broccoli and sauté
1 minute. Add the oyster-sauce mixture and stir well. Cook
only long enough to get it bubbling hot.

❨ SERVES 4.

Cauliflower and Ham

¾ *pound head of cauliflower*
3 *tablespoons vegetable oil*
⅓ *cup sliced raw ham*
2 *tablespoons soy sauce*
1 *tablespoon dry sherry*

½ *teaspoon salt*
2 *teaspoons cornstarch*
  mixed with 1 tablespoon
  water

Separate the cauliflower flowerets and cut each in half lengthwise. Drop in boiling water and parboil 1½ minutes. Drain, reserving ½ cup of the liquid. Heat a skillet, add the oil and sauté the ham ½ minute. Add the cauliflower, the reserved cauliflower liquid, soy sauce, sherry, salt, and cornstarch paste. Cook 1½ minutes.

◖ SERVES 3.

Green Beans with Pork

5 *tablespoons peanut or*
  vegetable oil
1 *slice ginger root or ¼*
  teaspoon ground ginger
½ *cup shredded lean pork*
  loin
½ *teaspoon soy sauce*
1 *tablespoon dry sherry*
¼ *teaspoon monosodium*
  glutamate

⅛ *teaspoon cornstarch*
¼ *teaspoon salt*
1 *pound fresh green beans,*
  cut in julienne strips
⅛ *teaspoon sugar*
½ *cup water*
1 *teaspoon cornstarch*
  mixed with 2 teaspoons
  water

Heat 3 tablespoons oil in a frying pan, add the ginger and the pork, which has previously been seasoned with the soy sauce, sherry, monosodium glutamate and ⅛ teaspoon cornstarch. Sauté 1 minute. In another frying pan heat the remaining oil, add the salt, beans and sugar and sauté 2 minutes. Add the water and bring to a boil. Cover and cook 4 minutes over medium heat. Thicken with the cornstarch paste. Combine with the pork, reheat and serve very hot.

(SERVES 4.

Desserts

9

Desserts

Peking Dust

1½ pounds chestnuts	1 cup heavy cream, whipped
6 tablespoons sugar	orange slices, preserved
½ teaspoon ground ginger	kumquats, glazed almonds
¼ teaspoon salt	or walnuts

Cut a crisscross on the top of each chestnut and cook the nuts in boiling water until shells burst and chestnuts are soft. Drain and remove shells. Force through a food mill. Mix in the sugar, ginger and salt. Fold in the whipped cream. Pack into a greased mold or bowl. Chill. Turn out and garnish with more whipped cream, the orange slices, kumquats and nuts.

❬ SERVES 6–8.

Steamed Ginger Cupcakes

2 eggs, separated	¼ teaspoon baking powder
½ cup powdered sugar	½ cup finely chopped
⅔ cup sifted flour	preserved ginger

Beat the egg whites until they form peaks. Gradually beat in the sugar until very stiff. Beat in the egg yolks. Sift the flour and baking powder over the mixture. Mix thoroughly. Fold in the ginger. Spoon mixture into 12 paper cupcake cups or greased glass custard cups. Stand on a rack in a large saucepan and add water to come just below level of rack. Cover, bring water to a boil and steam over low heat 20 minutes or until cakes are set. Serve hot or cold.

❲ MAKES 12.

Steamed Sponge Cake

4 *egg whites*
1 *cup sugar*
4 *egg yolks, beaten*
1⅓ *cups flour*
½ *teaspoon baking powder*

Beat the egg whites until soft peaks form, then gradually beat in the sugar until very stiff. Add the egg yolks, and beat again until thoroughly blended. Sift in the flour and baking powder and mix well. Pour into a lightly greased 8-inch-square baking pan. Place pan on a rack in a kettle or large saucepan and add boiling water to just reach the rack. Cover the kettle and steam 30 minutes or until cake is firm. Cut into squares and serve hot or cold.

❲ SERVES 6–8.

Eight Precious Pudding

1½ *cups raw long-grain rice*
½ *teaspoon salt*
5 *cups water*
1½ *cups sugar*
1 *cup chopped candied fruits*
1 *cup blanched almonds*
18 *pitted dates*
½ *cup seedless raisins*
1½ *tablespoons cornstarch*

Wash the rice, and combine with the salt and 4 cups water in a saucepan. Bring to a boil, cover and cook over low heat 20 minutes. Mix in ½ cup of the sugar. Arrange about ¾ of the fruits and nuts on the bottom of a greased 2-quart baking dish. Carefully pour the undrained rice over them, and arrange the remaining fruits and nuts on top. Tie a piece of parchment paper or aluminum foil over the top. Place dish on a rack in a deep pot. Add boiling water to just reach the rack. Cover the pot and steam over medium heat 30 minutes.

Prepare the sauce meanwhile. Mix the cornstarch with the remaining sugar and water. Bring to a boil, stirring steadily, then cook over low heat 5 minutes.

Carefully unmold the pudding, and pour the sauce over it.

(SERVES 8–10.

Gelatin-Fruit Dessert

2 *envelopes (tablespoons)* *gelatin*

4 *cups water*

3 *tablespoons sugar*

1⅓ *cups condensed milk*

2 *teaspoons almond* *extract*

1 *16-ounce can fruit* *cocktail*

Soften the gelatin in 1 cup of the water. Add the sugar and place over hot water, stirring until dissolved. Mix with the remaining water, the condensed milk and the almond extract. Pour into an oblong dish to a depth of 1 inch. Chill until set. Cut into fancy shapes with small cooky cutters, or into diamonds with a sharp knife. Mix with the undrained fruit cocktail and serve in sherbet glasses.

(SERVES 8–10.

Note: The fruit cocktail may be replaced by any fresh or canned fruit: mandarin oranges, peaches, strawberries. If desired, nuts may be added: lichee nuts, almonds, walnuts, etc.

Glazed Fruit

2 *apples*	3 *egg whites*
2 *bananas*	3 *cups vegetable oil*
4 *tablespoons cornstarch*	1 *cup sugar*
3 *tablespoons flour*	3 *tablespoons sesame seeds*

Peel the apples and cut each into 10 wedges. Peel the bananas and cut crosswise into 2-inch pieces. Mix together the cornstarch, flour and unbeaten egg whites until smooth. Dip the fruits in the batter, coating them well. Heat the oil in a skillet until it boils. Fry the fruits in it until delicately browned. Drain. Pour off all but ¼ cup oil. Add the sugar; cook over low heat, stirring constantly until sugar melts. Mix in the sesame seeds, then return the fruits. Baste and stir gently until fruits are covered with the syrup. Turn into a flat, hot dish. The fruits are served with a bowl of ice water for dipping, thus causing a glaze.

(SERVES 4–6.

Glazed Chestnuts

1 *pound chestnuts*	¾ *cup honey*
2 *cups sugar*	

Soak the chestnuts overnight in water to cover. Drain, shell, skin and dry. Combine the sugar and honey in a saucepan. Cook over low heat 1 hour, stirring frequently. Add the chestnuts and cook 2 hours, stirring frequently. Separate the chestnuts and let cool.

Fried Almond Custard

¼ *cup sesame seeds*   1 *cup water*
3 *egg yolks*   1½ *teaspoons almond*
4 *tablespoons sugar*   *extract*
½ *cup flour*   *vegetable oil for deep frying*
½ *cup cornstarch*

Brown the sesame seeds in a skillet, shaking the pan frequently to keep from burning. Pound or put through a Mouli grater. Reserve. Beat the egg yolks and 1 table-spoon sugar in a saucepan. Mix in the flour and 1 table-spoon cornstarch. Gradually stir in the water until smooth. Cook over low heat, stirring constantly until very thick. Pour into an oblong dish to a depth of ½ inch. Cool, then cut into strips. Dip in the remaining cornstarch. Heat the oil to 380° and fry the strips until browned. Drain. Sprinkle with the sesame seeds mixed with the remaining sugar.

◖ SERVES 4–6.

Almond Cookies

¼ *cup sugar*   1 *egg, lightly beaten*
1½ *cups sifted flour*   2 *teaspoons almond extract*
½ *teaspoon salt*   1 *egg yolk*
½ *teaspoon baking soda*   1 *tablespoon water*
⅓ *cup vegetable shortening*   *blanched almonds*

Sift the sugar, flour, salt and baking soda into a bowl. Work in the shortening by hand, then toss in the egg and almond extract until a ball of dough is formed. Shape into a roll about 1 inch in diameter. With a sharp knife, cut the roll in ½-inch slices. Arrange on a lightly greased cooky sheet, and flatten slightly. Beat the egg yolk and water and brush the tops of the cookies with it. Gently press an almond in the center of each cooky. Bake in a preheated 375° oven 10 minutes or until delicately browned.

◖ MAKES ABOUT 18.

Brown Sugar Cookies

1 cup rice flour	6 tablespoons soft butter
½ cup light-brown sugar	1 tablespoon ice water
2 cups finely ground blanched almonds	almonds for tops of cookies

Sift the rice flour and brown sugar into a bowl. Stir in the almonds. Work in the butter by hand. Mix in the ice water. Break off pieces of dough about the size of a tablespoon and form into balls. Arrange on a greased cooky sheet at 1-inch intervals. Flatten balls slightly and put an almond in the center of each. Bake in a 350° oven 10 minutes, or until delicately browned.

◖ MAKES ABOUT 30 COOKIES.

Peanut Candy

1 cup light corn syrup	3 cups coarsely chopped peanuts
1 cup brown sugar	
2 tablespoons butter	½ cup sesame seeds, toasted

Cook the corn syrup and brown sugar until a little dropped in cold water forms a hard ball (275° on a thermometer). Butter an 8-inch-square pan. Spread the peanuts and half the sesame seeds in it. Pour the syrup over it and sprinkle with the remaining sesame seeds. Cool and break into pieces.

◖ MAKES ABOUT 1 POUND.

Preserved Kumquats

1½ *pounds kumquats*
2 *cups water*
1 *cup sugar*
½ *cup preserved ginger,*
ground
3 *tablespoons lime juice*

Wash the kumquats in warm water; drain and dry. Gently prick each kumquat with a skewer in 2 or 3 places. Combine the water and sugar in a saucepan (not aluminum). Bring to a boil and add the kumquats. Cook over low heat 20 minutes, or until syrup is thick and clear. Stir in the ginger and lime juice. Pack in sterile jars and seal.

 ⟪ MAKES ABOUT 3 PINTS.

Chinese Fruit Bowl

½ *watermelon, cut*
crosswise
2 *cups melon balls*
1 *tablespoon lemon*
juice
1 *teaspoon grated lemon*
rind
1 *can fruit cocktail or an*
equal amount of diced
fresh fruit
2–3 *tablespoons sugar,*
to taste
1 *teaspoon lemon extract*
1 *teaspoon almond extract*

Scoop the flesh from the watermelon, forming it into balls. Notch the edge of the rind and dry the inside with paper towels. Sprinkle the melon balls with a mixture of the lemon juice and grated rind. Do not drain the fruit cocktail. (If you are using diced fresh fruit add 2 or 3 tablespoons sugar, to taste.) Mix all the fruits together with the lemon and almond extracts. Arrange in the watermelon rind set on crushed ice and chill thoroughly. Serve directly from the rind "bowl."

 ⟪ SERVES 8–10.

Note: Individual servings could be arranged in small melon halves. Mix the fruit in a large bowl and chill it, then spoon into the melon halves.

Menus

Menus

1

Spring Rolls · Duck Sauce, Chinese
Chicken Soup   Mustard
Sautéed Beef with Snow Peas · Boiled Rice
Chinese Fruit Bowl

2

Shrimp Toast · Duck Sauce, Chinese
Chinese Okra Soup   Mustard
Sweet and Sour Chicken · Boiled Rice
Steamed Ginger Cupcakes

3

Batter-Fried Shrimp · Duck Sauce, Chinese
Watercress Soup   Mustard
Chinese Fresh Ham · Boiled Rice
Peking Dust

4

Special Egg Fu-Yung
Cabbage Soup
Cubed Beef · Boiled Rice
Gelatin-Fruit

5

Eggs in Sweet and Sour Sauce
Wonton Soup
Steamed Beef Dumplings · Fried Rice
Preserved Kumquats

6

Egg Rolls · Duck Sauce, Chinese
Oxtail Soup   Mustard
Cantonese Lobster · Boiled Rice
Glazed Fruit

7

Spareribs with Pineapple
Sauce
Shrimp Soup · Boiled Rice
Duck Szechwan Style
Eight Precious Pudding

8

Asparagus with Ginger-Sherry
Sauce
Fried Fluffy Fish Balls
Velvet Chicken and Creamed
Corn · Chinese Bread
Glazed Chestnuts

Index

Index